"The best 'cliff notes' available for those new to consulting and an excellent refresher reference for the experienced."

Pamela J. Schmidt
Executive Director, ISA

"*The Consultant's Quick Start Guide*" begins and ends with the best questions available, and includes nine chapters in between of down-to-earth, easy-to-use information, advice, and guides to starting a successful consulting practice. By considering the chapter one questions of "assessing your consulting aptitude," you will have a clear idea of whether the profession is for you. And, if you answer affirmatively and start your own business, chapter eleven "brings it all together" by reviewing your first-year success in terms of personal, family, fun, and financial results. This is the one book that any new or aspiring consultant needs to quick start success."

Barbara Pate Glacel, Ph.D.
Author, *Light Bulbs for Leaders*
Principal, Glacel Developing Group

"This book is a must-have guide for consultants and provides powerful resources to help you 'practice what you preach' regarding the value of planful approaches to prosperity."

Debra A. Dinnocenzo
President, ALLearnatives
Author, *101 Tips for Telecommuters*

"Elaine Biech is right on the mark with her latest release: *The Consultant's Quick Start Guide.* With bookshelves full of numerous 'how-to' titles it is refreshing to find one that really is loaded with practical, easy-to-use information based upon Elaine's admirable consulting experience. If you are thinking of entering the consulting field and are looking for one easy-to-use manual, pick up a copy of *The Consultant's Quick Start Guide.*"

Joseph Ruppert,
Captain, USN, retired

"Elaine Biech has taken her many years of successful consulting expertise and graciously hands it over to new and seasoned consultants alike. Many seasoned folks would have saved a lot of time, money and sleepless nights if they had this when they started out."

Shirley Krsinich
Executive Talent Consultant, American Family Insurance Group

"If you really want to be a consultant, then this book is a must have. It takes you from A to Z, answering every question you may have about being a consultant. Like Elaine's previous books, *The Consultant's Quick Start Guide* provides practical, useful and simple advice and examples."

L. A. Burke
Quality Performance Consultant, 14th Coast Guard District

"Elaine Biech has done it again! A must for every aspiring entrepreneur, this book takes you by the hand and walks you through both a reality check and a process that will help you build the bridge between what you can dream and what you can accomplish."

Nancy A. Michaels
Executive Vice President, Great Circle Learning

"A must-read for people who are considering a career in consulting. The book is filled with realistic and practical ideas—a great way to learn all the tricks of the trade from one of the best!"

Vicki L. Chvala
Executive Vice President, American Family Insurance

"Anybody who wants to quit their day job to join the legions of free-agents and consultants needs this book. There are so many facets of the consulting business, and Elaine provides the quickest road to plan for success. This book will dramatically reduce your learning curve."

Kristin Arnold
President, Quality Process Consultants, Inc.

"An excellent guide for the new consultant just getting started. Also an extremely thorough checklist for the experienced consultant undergoing a process of career reevaluation. Guaranteed to help you answer the tough questions about how to succeed in this most challenging and rewarding of professions."

Jack R. Snader, C.M.C.
CEO, Systema Corporation

"*The Consultant's Quick Start Guide,* 2nd edition, is the best way I know to jump-start a successful career in consulting. Clearly written and imminently practical, this guide will save you countless hours of arduous toil. It is a virtual 'Vulcan mind meld' of collected wisdom, experience, and general business savvy. Bravo to Elaine Biech for this innovative tool kit for the consulting profession!"

Gary Muszynski
Creative Catalyst and Consultant, One World Music

"A logical, step-by-step guide through the consulting jungle. Follow Elaine's lead as if your business life was depending on it!"

Linda Byars Swindling
"The Peacemaker" and coauthor, *The Consultant's Legal Guide*

"Elaine Biech has done it again! For anyone considering leaving the corporate world to become a free agent, this practical book is enormously valuable. Even established consultants would do well to review and learn from Elaine's focused and efficient set of tools and principles. Save yourself a lot of time and effort—buy this book and use it before, during, and after you begin your consulting practice."

B. Kim Barnes
CEO, Barnes & Conti Associates, Inc.

"A quick start is no longer a luxury—it's a survival strategy! Elaine Biech's newest comprehensive resource can save you precious time and money when you need it the most. Learn from a 'master' who has built a very successful consulting business—you won't regret it!"

Ann Herrmann-Nehdi
CEO, Herrmann International

"If book titles could be lengthy, I would want to call this one: *How to Parachute into a Successful Consulting Practice Without Hitting a Tree or Landing in a Lake.* What a treat for the new or 'wannabe' consultant—you can think through the initial career decision, plan for the launch of the business, and hang the proverbial shingle with this book as your guide. The author has produced another practical, hands-on approach!"

Ronald E. Galbraith
CEO, Management 21, Inc.

The Consultant's

Quick

Start

Guide

An Action Plan
for Your First Year
in Business

Second Edition

elaine biech

Pfeiffer
A Wiley Imprint
www.pfeiffer.com

About Pfeiffer

Pfeiffer serves the professional development and hands-on resource needs of training and human resource practitioners and gives them products to do their jobs better. We deliver proven ideas and solutions from experts in HR development and HR management, and we offer effective and customizable tools to improve workplace performance. From novice to seasoned professional, Pfeiffer is the source you can trust to make yourself and your organization more successful.

Essential Knowledge Pfeiffer produces insightful, practical, and comprehensive materials on topics that matter the most to training and HR professionals. Our Essential Knowledge resources translate the expertise of seasoned professionals into practical, how-to guidance on critical workplace issues and problems. These resources are supported by case studies, worksheets, and job aids and are frequently supplemented with CD-ROMs, websites, and other means of making the content easier to read, understand, and use.

Essential Tools Pfeiffer's Essential Tools resources save time and expense by offering proven, ready-to-use materials—including exercises, activities, games, instruments, and assessments—for use during a training or team-learning event. These resources are frequently offered in looseleaf or CD-ROM format to facilitate copying and customization of the material.

Pfeiffer also recognizes the remarkable power of new technologies in expanding the reach and effectiveness of training. While e-hype has often created whizbang solutions in search of a problem, we are dedicated to bringing convenience and enhancements to proven training solutions. All our e-tools comply with rigorous functionality standards. The most appropriate technology wrapped around essential content yields the perfect solution for today's on-the-go trainers and human resource professionals.

www.pfeiffer.com

Essential resources for training and HR professionals

For Shane and Thad,

for giving me

my own Quick Start

Published by Pfeiffer
A Wiley Imprint
989 Market Street, San Francisco, CA 94103-1741 www.pfeiffer.com

Library of Congress Cataloging-in-Publication Data:

Biech, Elaine.
   The consultant's quick start guide: an action plan for your first year in business / Elaine Biech.—2nd ed.
      p. cm.
   Includes bibliographical references and index.
   ISBN 978-0-470-37231-9 (pbk.)
      1. Consulting firms—Management.   2. Business consultants.
   I. Title.   II. Title: Quick start guide.
   HD69.C6B5343   2009
   001—dc22

                                                   2008029695

Acquiring Editor: Matthew Davis   Production Editors: Michael Kay, Xenia Lisanevich
Director of Development: Kathleen Dolan Davies   Editor: Beverly H. Miller
Developmental Editor: Susan Rachmeler   Editorial Assistant: Lindsay Morton
Marketing Manager: Brian Grimm   Manufacturing Supervisor: Becky Morgan

Printed in the United States of America
PB Printing   10 9 8 7 6 5 4 3 2 1

Contents

11 So, Now What? Year Two and Beyond   215

Preface to the Second Edition

Why This Guide?

My recent book, *Business of Consulting, Second Edition,* provides readers with a great deal of practical advice for establishing a consulting business. It ends with the words, "Wish on paper, and it becomes a plan." This book, *The Consultant's Quick Start Guide, Second Edition,* provides the paper that you may use for wishing.

The Consultant's Quick Start Guide, Second Edition, can become your plan—your blueprint for a consulting start-up. It includes questions to stimulate your planning, worksheets to develop your plan, and ideas to keep you motivated and moving forward.

The second edition of this book has been updated with statistics, dates, and events related to consulting. New material has been added in several areas; there are now questions for other consultants, advice on office location options (including the option of no office at all), a list of electronic resources, and suggestions for a discussion with your boss.

Who Will Find This Guide Useful?

You will find this guide useful if you are thinking about trying your hand at becoming a consultant. This guide walks you through several issues you must consider in determining whether this profession is right for you. You will explore whether you have the required skills and attributes to be a successful consultant. You will rate yourself against other entrepreneurs. You will identify personal, professional, and financial considerations necessary to ensure a quick start. And you will also explore your preferred future to determine whether consulting will allow you to achieve your professional and personal life goals.

You may also find this guide useful if you are new to the consulting profession and want to upgrade your consulting business acumen. Perhaps you started your practice but didn't have time to develop a marketing plan. This guide presents questions for you to answer to create your marketing plan. New in the second edition is an overview of the ABCs of marketing to put that task in perspective. Perhaps you didn't take the time to put together a business plan, and now you find yourself heading in many directions at the same time and wondering whether there's a better way. The guide will walk you through the steps of developing a business plan. Perhaps you thought consulting would lead to more control of your life, but instead you find yourself drowning in paperwork and trying to balance a completely out-of-control schedule. The guide shares tips, tactics, and tools to bring both your paperwork and your schedule under control.

You will find this guide useful whether you have previously read *The Business of Consulting* or not. If you have, you will be prepared for many of the activities, assignments, and exercises you will complete in this book. And you will have read the practical advice and the real-world examples that support them. If you have not read *The Business of Consulting*, this condensed version provides a painless, fill-in-the-blank, practical approach to setting up your consulting business. This guide will take you through the highlights of establishing your consulting business. Nevertheless, you may still wish to purchase *The Business of Consulting* for a couple of reasons. If you need some of the forms discussed in this guide, you will find them on the CD that accompanies the other book. You may also want a more comprehensive treatment of the topic. To purchase a copy, you can go to any bookstore; you may order it from amazon.com; or you can purchase it directly from Jossey-Bass/Pfeiffer by calling 800/956–7739 or visiting the Web site at www.pfeiffer.com.

How to Use This Guide

I encourage you to write directly in this book. Although you may need a note pad to jot down some initial thoughts or to complete calculations, ample room has been provided for you to write most of your permanent plan directly on the pages.

This book has been designed for you to begin with Chapter One and work in order through the chapters to the end. Naturally you have your own unique needs, so you may wish to pick and choose the chapters (as well as the activities) that seem most pertinent to your situation. Of course, you will be the best prepared and most assured of success if you work through the entire guide.

If you are contemplating the consulting profession, I encourage you to begin with the activities in Chapters One and Two. They focus on planning your consulting future and will help you determine whether consulting is truly for you. You may also wish to work through those two chapters if you are already a consultant and not enjoying it as much as you anticipated.

Chapters Three and Four are critical to ensure that you spend enough time planning for a successful consulting practice. These chapters address business structure and revenue issues. Insurance has become more important since the first edition was published, so Chapter Four of the second edition has a list of questions to guide discussions with potential insurance agents. You'll also find an electronic resource to help you unravel the insurance mystery.

Chapter Five will walk you through developing your business plan. If you are already consulting and have skipped this step, it's never too late to go back and plan now. This guide's easy-to-follow question format makes putting your thoughts and ideas on paper as easy as possible.

Chapter Six is chock full of ideas for making the transition from an internal job to external consulting as painless as possible. New in this second edition is a list of suggestions for creating a discussion with your boss about your future plans.

Chapter Seven is all about your office: the whats, wheres, hows, and whys of running an efficient office. Working out of your home may seem like the easiest choice you have to make, but is it? Working out of your home has some definite advantages; it also has some disadvantages. If you are consulting and have made a decision about location, you may still want to read this chapter to determine whether you've thought of everything. For example, this edition offers ideas about planning for your technical requirements, such as electronic record keeping.

Chapters Eight and Nine focus on finding and acquiring clients. This information is worth reading at any stage of your business—unless you already have more work than you can handle. (And if that's the case, you may want to read Chapter Eight, "Growing Pains," in *The Business of Consulting*.) Marketing is a lot of common sense with a touch of creativity. Often simply reading someone else's ideas will remind you of what you knew all along but aren't practicing. These chapters will remind you again. This second edition includes a discussion of the kinds of elements you should consider for your Web site.

Chapter Ten is a lifesaver—both figuratively and literally. Surviving your first year of consulting is as much about the work you do as it is about the way you run the business and the way you take care of yourself. There's good advice here no matter how long you've been in business.

Chapter Eleven helps you focus on year two. Although you will not actually complete these exercises if you are just starting out, you may want to peek ahead to see what you will be expected to assess about your progress. A few modifications in the second edition to reviewing your first year with your family makes this chapter well worth your time.

The material in this guide will no doubt stimulate other thoughts and ideas. You may capture those thoughts at the end of each chapter on the Quick Start Lists. Space is available for you to list the actions you'll take based on what you read, the ideas that were stimulated by the chapter, and the questions you need answered. These lists summarize the actions you'll need to take to move forward.

To assist other consultants in getting started, I will compile ideas and lessons learned from consultants around the world and publish them in an upcoming *Pfeiffer Consulting Annual* or in a consultants' tips book. If you are interested in contributing, see the calls for submissions at the end of this book.

Now let's see what we can do to get you off to a quick start.

Acknowledgments

This book was "authored" by many wise and wonderful people, and I thank everyone who pitched in.

- Matthew Davis, my editor, for trusting me to meet deadlines and for regularly boosting my morale

- Cedric Crocker, my publisher, for wanting a second edition of this book for the Jossey-Bass/Pfeiffer family

- Susan Rachmeler, my developmental editor, for organizing, simplifying, suggesting, adding, and deleting material and encouraging me in the process

- Lorraine Kohart, my assistant, for keeping the rest of the world at bay and making up good excuses while I wrote

- Michael Kay and Xenia Lisanevich, production editors, for moving everything along to ensure meeting a tight production schedule

- Mentors—all of you—for believing in me always: L. A. Burke, Vicki Chvala, Linda Growney, Maggie Hutchison, Shirley Krsinich, Jean Lamkin, Mindy Meads, Pam Schmidt, Judye Talbot, and Kathy Talton

- Clients, for allowing me to learn from you as we work together

October 2008

elaine biech
ebb associates inc
Norfolk, Virginia

First Things First: Why Consulting?

In this chapter you will

- Define consulting
- Identify the experiences, skills, knowledge, and attributes that will lead you to a successful consulting career
- Assess your consulting aptitude
- Identify your initial consulting focus
- Test your entrepreneurial attitude

Consulting: What Is It?

A consultant is someone who provides unique assistance or advice to someone else, usually known as the *client*. The work is defined by the consultant's expertise, the structure in which the consultant works, and the process the consultant uses.

Expertise is based on what a consultant knows and has experienced. It can be anything from gardening to the stock market; from astral projection to pig farming; from organization development to preventing child abuse; from manufacturing to mining emeralds. In his book *Going Solo*, William J. Bond (1997) identifies a list of 296 specialty consulting fields. And his list does not include the eight I have listed in this paragraph.

The structure in which the consultant works can vary. You can work for a firm, for example, one of the large worldwide accounting firms, all of which have consulting branches. You could also work for a small or medium-size consulting firm or with a partner in an office. Other possibilities are working in a virtual organization with a loosely structured relationship with other consultants across states or even nations, working as a subcontractor to any of those I have listed, working by yourself from a home office, or any of a dozen other structures.

The process a consultant uses usually is within one of the steps of problem solving. For example, a consultant might help a client in these ways:

- *Identify the problem:* "Why aren't our catalogue sales growing the way we anticipated?" A consultant might identify the problem as wasteful use of resources or a lack of repeat business.

- *Identify the cause:* "What is causing limited repeat business?" A consultant might identify the cause as sales staff who are rewarded more for new than repeat business or as employees with poor customer service skills.

- *Identify the solution:* "How do we ensure that our employees have the skills they need?" A consultant might identify solutions such as hiring more highly skilled employees, offering higher compensation to attract and retain skilled employees, or using coaching to improve the customer service skills of current employees.

- *Implement the solution:* "How can we improve our employees' customer service skills?" A consultant might help implement a solution by designing and delivering customer service skills training, creating a mentoring program that encourages on-the-job skill sharing, or establishing a monitored customer call center that provides feedback to each employee.

To summarize, consultants' expertise, the structure in which they work, and the process they use define the work. And consultants' experiences usually lead them naturally to each of these three elements. Experience and education provide the expertise that leads them to the field in which they specialize. Experience in other organizations as well as the lifestyle a consultant chooses lead them to using the right consulting structure. And experience also provides the consultant with the process, usually based on what the consultant has used in past work or the process the consultant's company uses.

Why a Consulting Career?

No one should have to get up in the morning and go to work. Instead we should all be able to get up and go to play. That is, we should enjoy our work so much that it seems like play. Most of us, however, distinguish work (what we must do) from play (what we'd rather be doing). Unfortunately, most of us get up and go to work every morning and save what we'd rather be doing for later in the day or later in the week. Consulting affords the opportunity for your work to be what you'd rather be doing. How could that be? As a consultant you will have:

- The flexibility to determine when you work, where you work, with whom you work, and what kind of work you do

- The opportunity to use the skills, experience, knowledge, and expertise that you possess and enjoy using

- Control over how much money you will earn

- A chance to do more meaningful work, make a difference in the world, address that greater calling that comes from within

- An opportunity to travel

- The challenge to do more complex, exciting, or difficult work, to learn and grow

- The ability to live in a different location

Do any of these reasons resonate with you about why you would choose a consulting career?

Unfortunately, even when people are given a chance to create the kind of work they wish to pursue, they are sometimes unable to do so because there are so many choices. This book will help you begin to narrow those choices by identifying your experiences (opportunities for learning), your competencies (skills and knowledge), and your aptitude (natural talents and personal qualities).

So why are you interested in a consulting career? In the next sections you will explore the experiences, competencies, and attributes that will help define your consulting role. Let's begin by identifying the experiences you have had that would lead you to pursue a consulting career.

Explore Your Experiences

To begin to narrow your consulting choices, examine the expertise you've gained over the years. Although it's sometimes difficult to name your own expertise, you can easily identify experiences you've had. The skills and knowledge you've gained from your experiences helps define your consulting role. (We will further explore the structure you will consider in Chapter Four.)

Identify all the industries in which you have worked:

Identify all the volunteer experiences you've had:

Identify the organizational levels with which you have experience:

Rate your breadth and depth of experience:

Identify the experiences that were the most rewarding and enjoyable:

Identify the experiences that were the most negative and unpleasant and that you wish to avoid in the future:

The experiences you've had provide you with a level of expertise for which clients will pay. Later in this chapter, you will use the information you have filled in to begin to identify your consulting focus.

Inventory Your Competencies

Everyone is very skilled or very knowledgeable about at least one thing. My plumber, Owen, for example, is the most knowledgeable person I know about anything that goes wrong with my plumbing. He can diagnose problems over the telephone and is highly skilled at making a quick repair.

Identify the knowledge and information you have. For example, a computer salesperson knows about sales and probably has also learned time management skills; a nurse may have taken workshops and read several books to improve communication skills.

List the things you do better than most other people:

List the things that colleagues, employers, friends, and family say that you do better than most others:

Identify special classes, courses, or seminars you've taken:

List special certifications, licenses, credentials, or warrants you hold:

List the problem-solving processes in which you are competent—for example, team building, process improvement, root cause analysis, brainstorming, force field analysis, flowcharting, or dialogue facilitating:

List things you know a lot about:

The skills and knowledge you already possess will help you define your consulting role later in this chapter.

Skills and Knowledge Required of Consultants

From the following list, identify the skills and knowledge for which you require the most improvement. Check the three or four that will make the greatest difference as you begin your consulting role:

- ❏ Prospecting and marketing
- ❏ Diagnosing client needs
- ❏ Gathering data through interviews and surveys
- ❏ Improving processes
- ❏ Playing roles such as trusted adviser, change agent, or initiator
- ❏ Managing expectations
- ❏ Addressing resistance
- ❏ Managing and facilitating change
- ❏ Identifying mutual expectations
- ❏ Pricing projects
- ❏ Dealing with paperwork
- ❏ Analyzing business data

- ❑ Designing materials
- ❑ Solving problems
- ❑ Building relationships
- ❑ Communicating with others
- ❑ Writing proposals and reports
- ❑ Conducting training
- ❑ Facilitating meetings
- ❑ Coaching managers
- ❑ Knowledge of intervention models
- ❑ Knowledge of processes

Identify how you might gain the skills and knowledge you need:

Continuing to gain skills and knowledge is an investment in yourself. Every time you add to your knowledge base or increase your skills, you become more valuable as a consultant.

Assess Your Consulting Aptitude

Malcolm Forbes, publisher of *Forbes* magazine, has been credited with saying, "Too many people overvalue what they are not and undervalue what they are." Consulting takes a certain aptitude—those natural talents and personal qualities we all have.

It might be the ability to solve a problem methodically or the creative talent to see the problem as a solution. Don't underestimate your natural talents and abilities. And if you know your weaknesses, also know that you can overcome them.

Are You a Match for the Profession?

Read the following statements. They identify the aptitude, natural talents, and personal qualities it takes to be a consultant. Check all with which you agree:

❏ I am a hard worker.

❏ I am in good health.

❏ I am a risk taker.

❏ I have a thick skin; being called a pest, "beltway bandit," or con man does not bother me.

❏ I am persistent.

❏ I am a big-picture person.

❏ I pay attention to details.

❏ I am an excellent communicator—oral and written.

❏ I can think critically.

❏ I am an independent self-starter.

❏ I can promote myself.

❏ I can balance logic and creativity, big picture and details.

❏ I know my limitations.

❏ I can say no easily.

❏ I am self-disciplined.

❏ I am confident.

❏ I am flexible.

❏ I am a goal setter.

❏ I complete tasks.

❏ I am reliable and trustworthy.

❏ I like to work with people.

Although the number of statements you checked will not guarantee success as a consultant, the statements you did not check point to challenges you will face as a consultant.

Which natural talents and abilities need the most improvement and attention?

How will you adapt or acquire talents and aptitudes that aren't natural for you?

Pull It Together: Your Initial Consulting Focus

You have spent some time examining your experiences, your competencies, and your natural aptitudes. Now translate that into what a client might buy:

What experiences do you possess for which a client would be willing to pay?

What skills and knowledge do you possess for which a client would be willing to pay?

What natural talents and personal qualities do you possess for which a client would be willing to pay?

To what aspects of the problem-solving process would you be likely to contribute: identify the problem, identify the cause, identify the solution, or implement the solution?

What can you offer that will benefit clients? Check the items on this list that fit you, and then add several of your own.

❏ Diagnostic skills   ❏ Listening skills

❏ Analytical skills   ❏ Writing skills

❏ Research skills   ❏ Organizational skills

❏ Investigative skills   ❏ Change management experience

❏ Objectivity   ❏ Flexibility

❏ Creativity   ❏ New ideas

❏ Fast turnaround   ❏ Meeting deadlines

❏ My publications   ❏ My completed research

❏ My contacts   ❏ My patents

❏ Knowledge   ❏ Contacts with other experts

Experience with _____

_____

_____

Expertise in _____

_____

_____

Now take a first cut at describing your consulting work by completing the statement below. Some examples follow.

I am a_____consultant who helps

my clients to _____ .

This benefits them _____ .

Examples

"I am a process improvement consultant who helps my clients become more efficient. This benefits them by reducing redundancy, increasing quality, decreasing time spent, and reducing cost to the customer."

"I am a Web design consultant who helps my clients define and design Web sites. This benefits them by creating a professional-looking Web site in one-tenth the time and at half the cost."

Entrepreneur Attitude: Do You Have What It Takes?

In addition to the experience, competencies, and aptitudes that make up your expertise, you must realize that becoming a consultant means that you are joining the entrepreneurial ranks. The Entrepreneur Attitude Survey shown here will tell you whether you have what it takes to become an entrepreneur.

The Entrepreneur Attitude Survey

Instructions: Rate yourself on the following qualities. They represent the thinking of several authors about the requirements of a successful business owner. Spend ample time pondering these questions and answer honestly. Rate yourself on a scale from 1 to 4 as follows:

1 = strongly disagree   3 = agree
2 = disagree   4 = strongly agree

Circle your answers

1.	I usually try to take charge when I'm with others.	1	2	3	4
2.	I can do anything I set my mind to.	1	2	3	4
3.	I have a high tolerance for difficult situations.	1	2	3	4
4.	I believe I can always influence results.	1	2	3	4
5.	I am complimented on my ability to quickly analyze complex situations.	1	2	3	4
6.	I prefer working with a difficult but highly competent person rather than a friendly, less competent one.	1	2	3	4
7.	I can fire employees who are not producing.	1	2	3	4
8.	I'm willing to leave a high-paying, secure job to start my own business.	1	2	3	4
9.	I push myself to complete tasks.	1	2	3	4
10.	I can work long hard hours when necessary.	1	2	3	4
11.	I need to be the best at whatever I do.	1	2	3	4
12.	I do not become frustrated easily.	1	2	3	4
13.	I thrive on challenges.	1	2	3	4
14.	I become bored easily with routine tasks.	1	2	3	4

(Continued)

15. I dislike being told what to do. 1 2 3 4

16. I have a higher energy level than most people. 1 2 3 4

17. I have held numerous leadership positions. 1 2 3 4

18. I have the skills and enjoy accomplishing a
    complex task by myself. 1 2 3 4

19. I can change my course of action if something
    is not working. 1 2 3 4

20. I am seen as a creative problem solver. 1 2 3 4

21. I can balance the big picture and details of a
    business at the same time. 1 2 3 4

22. I can predict how actions today will affect
    business tomorrow and in the future. 1 2 3 4

23. I need at least _____ hours of   1 = 8 hrs   2 = 7 hrs
    sleep to function effectively.   3 = 6 hrs   4 = 5 or fewer hrs

24. I have at least ___ years of   1 = 1 yr   2 = 2 yrs
    experience in the business   3 = 3 yrs   4 = 4 yrs
    I will start.

25. Over the past three years   1 = 1–6 or more days   2 = 11–15 days
    I have missed a total of ___   3 = 6–10 days   4 = 0–5 days
    days of work due to illness.

Scoring: Total the numbers you circled.

90 to 100	Go for it!
82 to 89	Good chance of success
74 to 81	Pretty risky
73 and below	Better continue to collect a paycheck

Although this survey can give you a general picture of what it takes to be a successful entrepreneur, only you can decide whether the move is right for you:

What did you learn about yourself?

What concerns you the most about being an entrepreneur?

What obstacles might you need to overcome? How will you do that?

What strengths will you parlay to your benefit? How will you do that?

If your score was not as high as you would have liked it to be, call your local university or technical college to learn whether it offers classes in entrepreneurship. Ask for the reading list and syllabus. If you decide you do not wish to take such a course, you may at least want to read some of the books from the reading list to bolster your knowledge about what to expect.

Quick
Start  **ACTION**

A Baker's Dozen Questions to Ask a Consultant

Before you begin the next chapter, interview a consultant. Consider it your take-a-consultant-to-lunch assignment. Gain as much information as you can about what it's like to be a consultant. Use the following list of questions to start (and I'm certain you will come up with many others):

- How long have you been a consultant?
- How did you get started?
- Why did you decide to become a consultant?
- How would you describe your consulting practice and the business structure you've selected?
- What do you do for clients?

- What's a typical project like? A typical week?

- What are the work/life balance issues for a consultant, and how do you address them?

- What marketing activities do you conduct?

- What's the greatest challenge for you as a consultant? The most frustrating?

- What would you do differently if you could start your consulting practice over again?

- How can I best prepare myself to become a consultant?

- What would you miss the most if you quit consulting?

- What should I have asked about that I didn't?

● ●

After your interview, think about what you learned about consulting. How has it reinforced or changed your thoughts about consulting?

Now that you have defined consulting and identified the experience, skills, knowledge, and attributes that you have that will lead you to a successful consulting career, you are ready to plan that career. Use the Quick Start Lists on the next page to capture your thoughts before moving on to Chapter Two. You will find Quick Start Lists at the end of each chapter. As you read future chapters and identify items you wish to remember, turn to the back of that chapter and record the actions you want to take, the ideas you think of, and the questions for which you want answers.

Quick Start LISTS

Actions I Will Take

Ideas I Have

Questions I Have

Planning Your Consulting Future

In this chapter you will

- Explore your preferred future
- Determine whether consulting will lead you to your professional and personal life goals
- Identify personal, professional, and financial considerations to ensure a quick start
- Identify the changes you will need to make
- Create a personal expense plan

Your Preferred Future

Why do you wish to become a consultant? What is it about consulting that appeals to you? How will consulting lead you to your preferred future? It is important to explore why you want to become a consultant and in what ways you believe consulting will lead you to your preferred future. You are about to become an entrepreneur, and it is usually difficult to separate entrepreneurs from their businesses. Therefore, a plan for your consulting business should begin with a plan for you and your life. We touched on this in Chapter One. Now let's continue by describing your preferred future.

Describe Your Ideal Day

I remember working through this exercise twenty-two years ago in a two-week career exploration workshop. My descriptions went something like this: "I awaken naturally to the sound of the surf and smell of the early morning ocean breeze. I sip a cup of gourmet coffee on the deck for half an hour as I skim the morning paper. As inspiration overwhelms me, I move to my desk that overlooks the ocean to continue writing my latest novel. I am lost in the task and the time passes quickly until 2 P.M., when I stop for a walk along the beach. That evening I prepare for the client with whom I will work the next day."

At the time I was living on a dairy farm in the middle of Wisconsin with a small income from my fledgling consulting practice and no writing experience. I'm sure the people in the workshop with me were thinking, "Yeah, right! What a dreamer." Although I haven't written any novels yet, I do have over four dozen published books and articles to my credit, most written while gazing at the Atlantic Ocean or Chesapeake Bay, on which I own property.

Describe Your Future

Take some time now to describe your preferred future:

Describe your ideal day. How does your day begin? How will you divide your time? How does your day end?

Describe your surroundings. Where do you live? What do you see when you look out your window? What kind of car do you drive?

Describe your perfect job. What are you doing? With whom? Where are you working? What do clients say about your work? What do colleagues say about you?

Describe the logistics more thoroughly. How much do you travel? Where? How often? Who travels with you? What is your office like? Where is it? What's the view outside your office window?

Describe the results of your work. What honors or awards have you received? What's your annual salary? What profit does your business make? How much is in your retirement account? Your savings account?

What do you do for pleasure daily, weekly, and annually? With whom? Where? For what length of time? What hobbies have you tried?

What vacations have you taken?

What do you do when you're alone? What are you reading? What are your day-dreams?

What are your top five personal goals?

    1.

    2.

    3.

    4.

    5.

What are your top five professional goals?

1.

2.

3.

4.

5.

What are your top three to five financial goals?

1.

2.

3.

4.

5.

Will Consulting Lead You to Your Life Goals?

To determine whether consulting will help you reach your goals, you may begin by ensuring that you know why you want to become a consultant.

Why Are You Considering Consulting?

You probably have many reasons for your choice. Examine the three categories listed here and determine what part each plays in your decision. Think in terms of percentage. Divide 100 percent among the three categories. For example, if you just lost your job and consulting is the only answer you can see, you might rank "necessity" as 100 percent. If you have always wanted to be your own boss and you see an opportunity to consult in your present company, you might rank "personality" as 70 percent and "opportunity" as 30 percent. Place a percentage in the blank in front of each category that relates to your reasons.

_____ *It's a necessity:* You need a way to make a living and believe consulting offers that. Perhaps you prefer a 9-to-5 job but haven't found one; you can't find a match to your expertise in your locale; your experience is too specialized for available jobs; you're in a low-paying job and believe your expertise is worth more; you've been downsized out of a job; you've been laid off or fired; you see the writing on the wall and you need to take care of yourself; you've retired and want something to keep you busy; you want to pick up some extra cash, perhaps part time; or other reasons that necessitate making money as a consultant. Generally the reason is a desire for a job or the money that a job brings.

_____ *You see an opportunity:* You see a situation that you can exploit. Perhaps your company uses consultants, and you know you could do what they do, make more money, and work fewer days than you do now; you spot a trend in your field that is creating great demand for someone with your experience and skills; you have a special expertise for which there is a shortage; you have contacts, patents, or published works that you think are more valuable in another venue; consulting seems like an inexpensive and easy start-up; you want to travel; you want to live in a different location and see consulting as a way to get you there; or you see other unique options that could turn into business opportunities. Generally you could continue to do the job you are doing now, but want to take the risk.

_____ *Your personality demands it:* You want to consult. You would rather have your own business, no matter what the consequences. Perhaps you are disillusioned with your current employer and know you could do it better yourself; big business moves too slowly for you; you need a creative outlet; you want to make a difference and are not concerned about making as much money as you now make; you want to be independent; you want freedom from the daily grind; you want to be your own boss; you want to work on your own schedule in your chosen location; or other reasons for which you cannot work for someone else any longer. Generally you want to control your own destiny no matter what the impact on your lifestyle.

_____ *Other reasons:*

Your Responses and Things to Ponder

The reasons why you are considering a consulting career give you some things to think about. If you rated "necessity" highest, chances are that you will not be in consulting for very long. For some, consulting is just a temporary role until they get a "real job." You may not find that you have enough funds to satisfy both your personal and business needs. This can be a strain on you, your family, and your consulting business, making it difficult to persevere. Putting your personal savings and assets on the line for the business will probably be uncomfortable for you.

If you rated "opportunity" highest, you probably also recognize how short that opportunity may be. You will want to jump quickly to exploit it, but you must first complete the planning that is required. Don't put this book down until you have completed the work through Chapter Five at least. Your business plan should ensure that you have a focus on the future and help you to determine whether demand is increasing, fading, or being taken over by others.

If you rated "personality" highest, you are competitive and will do almost anything to ensure that your consulting business survives and then thrives. Your business plan may change rapidly as you continue to see new directions you want to go in. Don't forget to tell those around you about your new directions. Although you will work hard to be successful, be sure to allow time for the personal things in your life as well.

What do you want from consulting? How will consulting support the preferred future and lifestyle you identified earlier? Summarize what you have learned about yourself and your desires for the future.

Your Goals and Consulting

Return to your lists of goals on pages 22 and 23 and rank-order all of the goals you listed. List them in rank order below. Then specify how consulting will help or hinder your ability to achieve each goal.

Rank/Goal

1.

   Helps

   Hinders

2.

   Helps

   Hinders

3.

    Helps

    Hinders

4.

    Helps

    Hinders

5.

    Helps

    Hinders

6.

    Helps

    Hinders

7.

    Helps

    Hinders

8.

    Helps

    Hinders

9.

    Helps

    Hinders

10.

    Helps

    Hinders

11.

    Helps

    Hinders

12.

    Helps

    Hinders

13.

    Helps

    Hinders

14.

    Helps

    Hinders

15.

    Helps

    Hinders

Examine your rank ordering and reasoning. Does consulting do more to help or hinder you to achieve your goals? How do you feel about this?

Professional, Financial, and Personal Considerations

Becoming a consultant means that you will join the ranks of small business owners—entrepreneurs—as we discussed in Chapter One. Owning your own business is a major decision that will be a big change in your professional life and your family life. Capture your thoughts by answering the following questions. Then discuss your responses with your spouse, significant other, or other family members who will be affected by your decision.

Professional Considerations

What is the significance to you to give up your job, your title, and your affiliation with your current employer?

How will not having regular contact with colleagues affect your work?

How much of a risk do you consider it to be to start your consulting business? (Although the monetary risk is the first that people think of, there are other risks.)

How long and hard are you willing to work? (If consulting will be your primary source of income, it will require a sustained level of dedication and commitment of time to become profitable.)

What if you fail? How will you deal with failure?

Financial Considerations

How much money are you willing to invest in your consulting business?

How much of your savings are you willing to invest in your business?

How will your retirement be affected if you move into consulting?

How do you feel about paying for your own dental and medical insurance?

How will you react when a client does not pay on time?

How will you react if you do not meet your financial goals? (It's not unusual to work with an organization for months to line up a project, only for the deal to fall through at the last minute.)

Do you have other financial resources? If required, would it be a financial hardship to you and your family to use these resources?

Personal Considerations

How will your business affect your personal life?

How much time and energy are you willing to invest in your business, and how will this affect your personal life? (Expect sixty to eighty hours per week during the first year.)

How do you feel about delaying dinner, missing a Saturday trip to the zoo, or skipping a family vacation because a project took longer than you anticipated?

What's more important to you: your family or your business? How will you demonstrate this?

Identify the Changes You Will Need to Make

Only you can determine if the time is right for you to make the switch to consulting. To help you make that decision, think about the changes you will have to make. Begin to list those changes here.

Professional Changes

Moving out on your own has professional implications. What changes will you have to make in your lifestyle to accommodate your needs as a professional?

Financial Changes

What changes will you make to your financial situation so that you can continue the lifestyle you have now? Or will you adjust your lifestyle and, if so, how?

Personal Changes

Without someone assigning your hours, you will have to manage your time to ensure that you take time off: nights, weekends, vacations. Do you see any changes that you will have to make to ensure a balanced lifestyle?

Create Your Personal Expense Plan

In upcoming chapters, you will create financial statements for your business. Based on what you have read in this chapter, you can see that you will want to have a good grasp on your personal living expenses. Use the process below and the Personal Expense Plan to assist you.

1. Estimate your personal expenses for the next year. The easiest way to do this is to analyze your checkbook for the past year. Don't forget to include expenses on your credit card statements too. Remember to think about unforeseen expenses that may occur. It's always better to plan for the worst scenario. Identify income and expenses for each month.

2. Analyze your savings, and decide exactly how much you are willing to invest in the business. Many business planners recommend that you have at least six to twelve months of living expenses in your savings account. This of course does not mean that you should plan to spend all of it before you are successful.

3. Estimate what you will withdraw from savings and how much income you believe you will receive from the business each month.

4. Summarize the data on a twelve-month personal expense plan.

5. Recognize that this is only your rough estimate at this time. In upcoming chapters, you will identify start-up costs, financial targets for the business, and other financial information that will provide a more accurate picture. You will want to return to this form later. For now, however, it does give you an idea of your personal income and spending pattern.

● ●

This exercise provided a projection of your personal budget. Chapter Three leads you through several exercises that will help you anticipate your professional consulting budget.

Personal Expense Plan

	Jan	Feb	Mar	April	May	June	July	Aug	Sept	Oct	Nov	Dec	Full Year
Expenses:													
Food													
Clothing													
Mortgage/Rent													
Utilities													
Electricity													
Heat													
Telephone													
Entertainment													
Automobile													
Payment													
Repairs/Maintenance													
Insurance													
Medical													
School Expenses													
Child Care													
Dues													
Major Purchases													
Property Taxes													
Other Taxes													
Monthly Totals													
Income:													
Spouse/Other Income													
Cash from Business													
Savings Withdrawal													
Additional Cash Required													

Source: The Consultant's Quick Start Guide: An Action Plan for Your First Year in Business, Second Edition. Copyright 2009 by John Wiley & Sons, Inc. Reproduced by permission of Pfeiffer, an Imprint of Wiley. www.pfeiffer.com (originally from Biech, 2007).

Quick Start LISTS

Actions I Will Take

Ideas I Have

Questions I Have

Dollars and Sense

3

In this chapter you will

- Establish a start-up budget
- Establish your pricing structure
- Calculate the revenues you will require
- Complete financial forms such as revenue projections, cash flow sheets, and expense records

Establish a Start-Up Budget

Identify everything you will need to start your consulting practice. Think in terms of furniture, equipment, supplies, occupancy costs, and setup expenses.

You may wish to go to your local office supply store and place an order for everything you think you will need. However, before you do that, consider how you could acquire the same items with a smaller outlay of cash. Look around your house. Do you have a table or chairs or bookshelves that you could borrow temporarily? Look around your neighborhood. Could you watch the ads for garage sales that might have desks or telephones? We found a fabulous solid oak desk for our receptionist that was advertised in an employee's church bulletin for forty-five dollars. Watch for offices that are moving or going out of business. You will find fabulous bargains and things you never knew you needed!

Calculate how much you will need to start your business. Starting a business is an iterative process (even though it may sometimes feel as if everything has to be completed at once). Therefore, you may not be able to complete all the blanks yet. For example, you will not explore your insurance requirements until the next chapter. Yet even though you do not know the exact cost of everything, it is important that you begin to identify what you will need and estimate as closely as you can how much you will need to invest. Later, when you have a better idea of your insurance requirements, you will be able to estimate the cost more closely.

Identify where you will beg, borrow, and shop to fill your start-up list. Identify the item, the person, or company from whom you will obtain it, and their telephone numbers or e-mail addresses. Then use the Start-Up Expenses form to organize your thoughts about what you will need and how much it should all cost.

What I Need   *Who I'll Call*

Communication/telephone equipment

Furniture

Computer, printer, and other equipment

Office and seminar supplies

Marketing supplies

Legal support

Accounting support

Banking support

Insurance support

Licenses and permits

Office space

Home office remodeling

Utilities hook-ups

Web site design

Answering, printing, transcription, or graphic services

Start-Up Expenses

	Estimated Cost
Furniture	
Desk and chair	$_____
Filing cabinet	$_____
Bookcases	$_____
Table	$_____
_____	$_____
_____	$_____
Equipment	
Computer	$_____
Software: _____	
_____	
_____	$_____
Printer/scanner	$_____
Copier	$_____
Fax machine	$_____
Adding machine, calculators	$_____
Telephone system	$_____
Answering machine	$_____
Cell phone, pager, BlackBerry	$_____
Postage scale	$_____
Postage meter or online postage service	$_____
_____	$_____
_____	$_____
Office Supplies	
Stationery	$_____
Paper: Printer	$_____
Specialty	$_____
Three-hole punch	$_____
Daily planner or PDA	$_____
Pens, pencils	$_____
Tape, glue, other adhesives	$_____
Scissors, rulers, miscellaneous	$_____

Start-Up Expenses, Cont'd

	Estimated Cost
Seminar Supplies	
Pocket folders	$_____
Three-ring binders	$_____
_____	$_____
_____	$_____
Marketing Supplies	
Web site	$_____
Business cards	$_____
Brochures	$_____
Printed pocket folders	$_____
_____	$_____
_____	$_____
Corporate Setup Fees	
Professional fees	$_____
Legal fees (incorporation)	$_____
Business name search	$_____
Accounting fees	$_____
Banking start-up	$_____
Insurance	$_____
Licenses/permits	$_____
_____	$_____
_____	$_____
Occupancy Costs	
Rent deposit	$_____
Utilities deposit	$_____
Answering service	$_____
_____	$_____
_____	$_____
Personal Living Expenses	
Remodeling: accommodate office	$_____
Moving van	$_____
_____	$_____
_____	$_____
Unanticipated Expenses	
_____	$_____
_____	$_____

Source: The Consultant's Quick Start Guide: An Action Plan for Your First Year in Business, Second Edition. Copyright 2009 by John Wiley & Sons, Inc. Reproduced by permission of Pfeiffer, an Imprint of Wiley. www.pfeiffer.com (originally from Biech, 2007).

Put a Price on Your Head

This is the best part of this guide! You get to name your price! What will it be? $175 per hour? $250 per hour? $1,500 per day? $40,000 per project? But why would a client pay you all that money? Are you worth it? Let's begin by exploring why you may be a good investment for your clients—and worth every dollar they pay you. Then let's move on to determine what that dollar value will be.

Five Reasons Why You May Be a Good Investment

As technology, information, and workloads surge, so does the demand for consultants. Consulting projects have dramatically increased in recent years. All the good consultants I know have more work than they can handle. I believe there are at least three reasons behind this.

First is the trend toward outsourcing more and more services. Corporations continue to hire more temporary professionals to assist when needed, as opposed to adding highly paid permanent staff. Consultants can temporarily provide the people power to complete the work at the time it needs to be completed, allowing organizations to avoid long-term costs or commitments.

Second, the exodus of the baby boomers is finally upon us. In no other time in history has there been an event that has marked the workforce so keenly. Without the knowledge of this powerful group, companies may struggle just to sustain their current abilities. According to some estimates, 35 to 40 percent of the nation's workforce is currently poised for retirement. Add to that the fact that the number of people in the U.S. workforce ages thirty-five to forty-five will actually decline by 10 percent, and you have a potential workforce crisis unfolding. Many organizations are prepared to lose one-fifth of their executives, managers, and other employees who have critical skills by 2015. This is an opportunity for consultants (some made up of the same retirees who want to work part time) to help companies fill in the gaps.

The third is related to the rapid technological changes occurring in the world. The explosion of knowledge and fast pace of communication make it nearly impossible for an executive team to remain completely knowledgeable about its industry, focused on the customers, and ahead of the competition; and the team may not know instantly what to do when these factors collide. Consultants offer the knowledge, information, data, and systems to solve the puzzle.

So why would your clients pay your high prices? You may offer at least five value-added reasons.

1. You may have the experience, expertise, and time that your clients' employees do not. Managers are bombarded daily with new projects that require new skills and more time. In today's fast-paced, ever-changing environment, organizations have difficulty hiring enough good people just to keep up with normal, ongoing tasks. Adding the fast-paced changes to the retirement conundrum, organizations may turn to you to fill the knowledge and time gap for the many special projects that arise. You will bring experience and expertise from past projects and other organizations.

2. You may provide flexibility for your clients. They may see you as someone who can be brought in for short-term projects. This is especially true if they have not planned for fast-paced changes in projects and people. You will be there when they need you and gone when they don't. Your clients will see that you will work beyond the forty-hour week to get the job done. Unlike hired staff, who require ongoing paychecks, benefits, and severance packages, consultants serve their purpose and then they are gone.

3. You may offer a fresh, objective point of view. With hundreds of other projects under your belt and valuable experience in dealing with an array of situations and personalities, you will be able to provide unbiased, fresh ideas. You will bring ideas and experiences from other firms and industries. This cross-pollination is a surefire way to tap into the brain power of many resources. Staff may be too close to the problem to see the solution. In addition, you will not be influenced by the internal politics that may prevent employees from telling the emperor he has no clothes.

4. You will most likely be more efficient for three reasons. First, you bring experience with similar problems and do not need to get up to speed. Second, you have the luxury of focusing solely on the assigned project or problem, unlike employees who have to complete their normal jobs while working on special projects. Third, you do not need to deal with the organization's internal politics and daily tasks: staff meetings, time and attendance records, retirement parties, e-mails, and other policies and procedures. You will arrive, put your head down, and get to work. Is it any wonder that a consultant can get a project completed in one-fourth the time of an in-house employee?

5. You may offer proof of honest endeavor. When other parties are involved, you may serve as a sign that an effort is in progress. For example, during a merger or other organizational change, you might serve as an independent mediator to resolve differences. At other times, organizations may find that they are not in compliance with environmental or safety laws. You may be hired for your expertise to show that an effort has been made to correct the problem.

When it comes to the bottom line, consultants are often more cost-effective for an organization. Organizations may hire you to gain skills on an as-needed basis rather than training and educating internal staff with skills that may not be used again. You can provide the solution many organizations are looking for. You will have the skill, time, experience, and expertise to get the job done; you can offer an independent perspective and insight; you will be fair, honest, and ethical; and best of all, there will be no ongoing salary, payroll taxes, benefits, or equal employment opportunity complaints.

Now summarize the value you could add for your client:

- Do you have experience or expertise that you could implement immediately?

- Can you provide flexibility to complete short-term projects?

- Can you offer a fresh, objective point of view?

- Can you be more efficient as a consultant than an employee?

- Do you have unique expertise that may not be found inside organizations?

Write a short paragraph responding to these questions to assure yourself that you will add value for your clients.

Calculate Required Revenue

As you determine what to charge your clients, you will need to keep two questions separate:

- How much money do you need?
- How much will clients be willing to pay you?

Although they are related, they are different. If your client is willing to pay more than you need, you should not hesitate to move forward. On the other hand, if you need more money than you think a client would pay, you might want to reconsider a career as a consultant. We will be concerned primarily with uncovering the numbers in this chapter. If you want a more in-depth rationale and discussion, turn to the "Dollars and Sense" chapter in *The Business of Consulting*.

How Much Money Do You Need?

You can determine how much income you will need in two ways.

First, you may calculate in detail your salary, taxes, benefits, and business expenses for one year. This will give you a more accurate calculation and a better prediction than the other method of where your money will be spent than the second method. The downside is that it is more time-consuming.

Second, you can use what I call the "3× Rule" (pronounced "three times rule"). This is a fast and relatively accurate estimate. The downside is that it will not provide you with the detail you may want as a start-up business.

Both are provided here. You may wish to do both and then compare the final numbers. If you are serious about moving into consulting, I recommend that you use the calculation method because this is an important step in your planning. If you are still in the exploratory stages of a consulting career, the 3× Rule will serve you well for now.

- **The calculation method:** Most of us relate our value to the salary that we draw. Use Calculating What you Require on page 47 to identify your salary, benefits, taxes, and business expenses for one year. If it's difficult for you to identify the exact cost of your benefits because you do not have all the data at this time,

Calculating What You Require

Your Salary for One Year _____

Your Benefits

Health insurance _____
Life insurance _____
Disability insurance _____
Retirement _____

Total Benefits _____

Taxes

Self-employment _____
Social Security and Medicare _____
State income tax _____
City tax _____
Personal property tax _____

Total Taxes _____

Business Expenses

Accounting, banking, and legal fees _____
Advertising and marketing _____
Automobile expenses _____
Books and resources _____
Clerical support _____
Copying and printing _____
Donations _____
Dues and subscriptions _____
Entertainment _____
Equipment leases _____
Insurance: _____
  Casualty
  Liability
  Professional liability
Interest and loan repayment _____
Licenses _____
Lodging (nonbillable) _____
Meals _____
Office supplies _____
Postage _____
Professional development _____
Rent _____
Repairs and maintenance _____
Telephone _____
Travel (nonbillable) _____
Utilities _____

Total Business Expenses _____

Total Required _____

Source: The Consultant's Quick Start Guide: An Action Plan for Your First Year in Business, Second Edition. Copyright 2009 by John Wiley & Sons, Inc. Reproduced by permission of Pfeiffer, an Imprint of Wiley. www.pfeiffer.com (originally from Biech, 2007).

you can estimate them at 33 percent of your salary. Remember when you begin to fill in the expenses that they are for one full year of operation but do not include one-time start-up expenses.

● **The 3× Rule:** If you do not wish to spend the time identifying all your business expenses, the 3× Rule gives a close approximation. Many consulting firms use this rule to determine how much to invoice clients for services. It also serves as a guide to know how much consultants should generate to cover their salaries. For example, consultants with a salary of $90,000 are expected to bill (and in many firms generate, too) at least three times that amount, or $270,000. Does that seem excessive? Why is it that high? Of course, $90,000 is paid in salary. The rest is necessary to cover fringe benefits, such as insurance, FICA, unemployment taxes, workers' compensation, and vacation time; overhead, such as advertising, rent, professional development, telephone, supplies, clerical support, and management; down time, including days when consultants are traveling, on vacation, or in training; and development and preparation time. In addition, any good business should be looking for a profit. If it is publicly held, its shareholders expect it. You will consider profit margins in Chapter Eleven.

As a start-up company working from your home, you may consider something closer to a 2× or 2½× Rule. I do caution you, however, not to cut it too closely. Your budget will be tight and you may experience cash-flow problems. For now, aim for an income for your business that is three times the salary you will draw. Figure that out here:

Your Salary $_____ × 3 = $_____

Determining Actual Billable Days

The next step is to identify how many billable days you expect to have in one year. The answer is not as easy as you might expect. Begin by answering the following questions:

How much time will you take off for vacations?

How much time off will you allow for illness or personal emergencies?

Do you plan to work weekends?

How much time do you need for administrative work?

How much time will you need for marketing?

How much other down time do you expect to encounter?

Once you've answered these questions, fill in the following chart to determine your actual billable days.

Days in a Year	365
Weekend Days	−104
	=261
Time Off	
Vacation, personal (5 to 15 days per year)	− _____
Holidays (6 to 12 days per year)	− _____
	= _____
Marketing (1 to 2 days per week)	− _____
Administrative (2 to 4 days per month)	− _____
	= _____
Down time (15 to 30 percent)	− _____
Days you expect to work	_____

Calculating a Daily Fee

Now let's put the two figures together. Divide what you require by the number of days you expect to work to identify your daily fee. If you expect to charge by the hour, divide that by eight.

What you require/Days you expect to work = Daily Fee

$ _____   /   _____ days   = $ _____ per day

Calculating an Hourly Fee

Daily Fee / 8 Hours = Hourly Fee

_____ / 8 Hours = $ _____ per hour

How do you feel about the amount you have identified?

How Much Will Clients Pay?

Ultimately the client determines acceptable fee ranges. The factors that determine how much a client will pay fall into two categories. The first is the client: the industry, the size, location, demand, and reliance on the consultant in the past. The second is the consultant: level of expertise, time in the consulting field, stature in the profession, name recognition, and area of expertise. I've worked with consultants who have charged as little as $200 per day and with those who charge as much as $55,000 for a one-hour speech.

To determine whether you will charge at the high end or the low end, compare the following pairs of descriptions. Place an X in either the left or right column next to the one that more closely describes you and your potential clients. This is certainly not a foolproof way to determine what you will charge. It does, however, give you more information.

My Consulting

____ Expertise in high demand	____ Minimal demand for expertise
____ Over 20 years in industry	____ Under 10 years in industry
____ High name recognition	____ No name recognition
____ Area of specialty rare	____ Specialty readily available
____ Fills a gap in the workforce	____ Skills/knowledge easily accessible
____ Published work is well known	____ No published work

My Clients

____ High-paying industry	____ Low-paying industry
____ For profit	____ Nonprofit
____ Large companies	____ Small companies
____ Large city	____ Small town
____ Coast locations	____ Midwest
____ High use of consultants	____ Minimum use of consultants
Totals_____	_____

Total the Xs in each column. The more Xs you have in the left column, the higher rate you will be able to charge.

Quick Start ACTION

Setting Your Fee

Check the competition. Before moving forward, check your market area for services similar to yours and identify what they are charging. For example, a local mental health clinic may offer a stress management class for $25. Your local community college may offer on-site support for identifying corporate computer needs at $75 per hour. A local training, consulting, or facilitation association chapter may offer facilitation as a community service. If any of these is similar to what you offer, you may have a difficult time convincing companies to pay $1,200 per day for your services—even if you do customize the materials for them. Start with the Yellow Pages. Then make a few telephone calls to members of your network. Jot down any information you learn below.

And the Number Is ...

You've calculated, contemplated, researched, and studied. It's time to put the figure on paper.

The fee I will charge clients is:

$ _____ per _____

• •

Fill Out Financial Forms

Although it might seem early in the process to begin to think in terms of a budget and cash flow projections, the truth is that it can never be too early to project what it will take to manage the finances of your business. The next three forms will help you do that.

The Budget Form provides a way for you to list all expenses you expect for the year. The First-Year Cash-Flow Projection form will help you organize the flow of money coming in and going out the first year. Cash flow is critical and is often a key reason that businesses fail: they can't pay their bills. This happens because there is a delay between expenses you incur for a project and the income you will receive from it.

For example, you may complete a project during the month of May, incurring copying, travel, and overhead costs. You will probably bill the client for your work around June 1. It may take three to five days for your invoice to reach the client's accounts payable department. Most companies wait until the last minute to pay their bills. (This helps their cash flow situation and allows them to collect interest as long as possible—something you will most likely do as well.) You may not receive a check for your work until the middle of July. And that's the positive scenario. Your invoice could be lost in the mail or in the client's system. The check could get lost on its way to you. In the meantime, you have those expenses incurred in May to pay.

As you complete your cash flow projections, I recommend that you think practically and plan generously so you are less likely to be caught in a cash flow crunch.

The Three-Year Cash Flow Projection form gives you the same perspective but for a longer period of time. It is also more general. Think three years out. How profitable will you be by then?

Budget Form

Net Salary for One Year ⎯⎯⎯⎯

Benefits
    Health insurance ⎯⎯⎯⎯
    Life insurance ⎯⎯⎯⎯
    Disability insurance ⎯⎯⎯⎯
    Retirement ⎯⎯⎯⎯

Total Benefits ⎯⎯⎯⎯

Taxes
    Self-employment ⎯⎯⎯⎯
    Social Security and Medicare ⎯⎯⎯⎯
    State income tax ⎯⎯⎯⎯
    City tax ⎯⎯⎯⎯
    Personal property tax ⎯⎯⎯⎯

Total Taxes ⎯⎯⎯⎯

Business Expenses
    Accounting, banking, legal fees ⎯⎯⎯⎯
    Advertising and marketing ⎯⎯⎯⎯
    Automobile expenses ⎯⎯⎯⎯
    Books and resources ⎯⎯⎯⎯
    Clerical support ⎯⎯⎯⎯
    Copying and printing ⎯⎯⎯⎯
    Donations ⎯⎯⎯⎯
    Dues and subscriptions ⎯⎯⎯⎯
    Entertainment ⎯⎯⎯⎯
    Equipment leases ⎯⎯⎯⎯
    Insurance ⎯⎯⎯⎯
    Interest and loan repayments ⎯⎯⎯⎯
    Licenses ⎯⎯⎯⎯
    Lodging (nonbillable) ⎯⎯⎯⎯
    Materials (nonbillable) ⎯⎯⎯⎯
    Meals ⎯⎯⎯⎯
    Office supplies ⎯⎯⎯⎯
    Postage ⎯⎯⎯⎯
    Professional development ⎯⎯⎯⎯
    Rent ⎯⎯⎯⎯
    Repairs and maintenance ⎯⎯⎯⎯
    Salaries (employees) ⎯⎯⎯⎯
    Seminar expenses ⎯⎯⎯⎯
    Telephone ⎯⎯⎯⎯
    Travel (nonbillable) ⎯⎯⎯⎯
    Utilities ⎯⎯⎯⎯

Total Business Expenses ⎯⎯⎯⎯
Total Required for One Year ⎯⎯⎯⎯

Source: The Consultant's Quick Start Guide: An Action Plan for Your First Year in Business, Second Edition. Copyright 2009 by John Wiley & Sons, Inc. Reproduced by permission of Pfeiffer, an Imprint of Wiley. www.pfeiffer.com (originally from Biech, 2007).

First-Year Cash-Flow Projection

	Jan	Feb	March	April	May	June	July	Aug	Sept	Oct	Nov	Dec
Revenue												
Total Revenue												
Expenses												
Accounting/banking/legal												
Advertising/marketing												
Automobile												
Benefits												
Books/resources												
Clerical support												
Copying/printing												
Donations												
Dues/subscriptions												
Entertainment												
Equipment leases												
Insurance												
Interest												
Licenses												
Lodging												
Materials												
Meals												
Office supplies												
Postage												
Professional development												
Rent												
Repairs/maintenance												
Salaries												
Seminar expenses												
Taxes												
Telephone												
Travel												
Utilities												
Total Expenses												
Monthly Cash Flow												
Cumulative Cash Flow												

Source: The Consultant's Quick Start Guide: An Action Plan for Your First Year in Business, Second Edition. Copyright 2009 by John Wiley & Sons, Inc. Reproduced by permission of Pfeiffer, an Imprint of Wiley. www.pfeiffer.com (originally from Biech, 2007).

Three-Year Cash-Flow Projection			
	Year 1	Year 2	Year 3
Total Revenue	_____	_____	_____
Expenses:			
Salaries	_____	_____	_____
Benefits	_____	_____	_____
Taxes	_____	_____	_____
Marketing	_____	_____	_____
Administrative/Overhead	_____	_____	_____
Total Expenses	_____	_____	_____
5 Percent Inflation	no*	_____	_____
Expenses + Inflation	no*	_____	_____
Projection	_____	_____	_____
(Revenue – Adjusted Expenses) After Inflation	_____	_____	_____

*No inflation is added the first year.

Source: The Consultant's Quick Start Guide: An Action Plan for Your First Year in Business, Second Edition. Copyright 2009 by John Wiley & Sons, Inc. Reproduced by permission of Pfeiffer, an Imprint of Wiley. www.pfeiffer.com (originally from Biech, 2007).

So What's It Take to Get off the Ground?

What Will It Cost?

Running a business means that you must pay your bills every month. So after all the numbers we've just run through, what's it really going to take to get started? How much money will you need?

The total cost is actually a combination of two things. The first is your start-up costs. These are one-time costs to open your business, and you won't encounter many of them again. Some, like insurance, will be due on a quarterly or semiannual basis. Others, like the desk you borrowed from Aunt June and the scratch-and-dent bargain you picked up at the surplus store, will not cost anything again until you replace them.

Where Will I Find the Money?

Some financial advisers recommend that you have six months' living expenses saved. Others recommend a full year. It really depends on you and whether you have a supplemented income or whether you can tighten your belt. You can use your estimated living expenses from Chapter Two to judge whether you have sufficient savings.

If you have decided to move forward and do not have all the money you need, you will spend time examining your dilemma in Chapter Six. Now let's depart from the financial discussions and identify other aspects of starting your business in the next chapter.

Quick Start LISTS

Actions I Will Take

Ideas I Have

Questions I Have

Taking Care of Business

4

In this chapter you will

- Name your business
- Learn how to find the best accountant and attorney
- Determine the best business structure for your situation
- Explore your banking and insurance needs
- Check zoning laws, licenses, and taxes for which you will be responsible
- File legal documentation
- Create a to-do list to organize all that needs to be completed to get your business started

Getting Started

You've probably figured out by now that there are many tasks to getting a business started and off the ground. If you have been working through the tasks along the way, you have completed a great deal of the preliminary work that will prepare you for this chapter. You will find a to-do list at the end of this chapter that will remind you of everything that needs to be completed at this stage. Let's begin by determining what you want to call your consulting business.

What's in a Name?

Selecting your business name requires two important considerations. First, you want to select a name that is easy to remember so your clients will remember to call you. Second, select a name that is professional and establishes your image. If you can also select a name that says what you do, all the better. Your business name is the first image you present to your clients.

The name you select for your business will have strong implications for how your clients view you and your business. For example, you might choose to use your name. The advantage of "Joe Bloomer Consulting" is that it tells potential clients who you are and the nature of your business. The drawback is that it limits your clients' perception of your business to one person. Joe may have ten people working for him, but the name will prevent that information from readily surfacing.

What is your vision for the future of your consulting business? Will you have employees? Associates? Partners? Your name should allow for your future growth or challenge. Many consultants use "Joe Bloomer and Associates" or "The Bloomer Group" even though Joe may be starting out on his own. That way, they are prepared for adding others as they grow the business.

The drawback of using your name in any configuration is that you identify yourself as the head person, and this may be seen negatively by colleagues who may want to join you in your consulting business. But if you have strong name recognition, such as "The Ken Blanchard Companies," using your name can be an advantage to both finding clients and hiring people.

Some consultants choose the name of their business's location as a name. Some names may sound great, but you will need to determine whether they also might be limiting. "The Northwest Group" sounds impressive and conjures up great graphics, but will companies in the Midwest and the Southeast consider hiring you? And consider this one: "Herrmann International" is the ultimate in not limiting yourself to one locale.

Select a name that exudes a professional image and, if possible, tells the client what you do. "Bloomer Executive Coaching" or "Team Solutions" tells potential clients what you do. At the minimum, your company name should not confuse clients. Take care, however, that you do not get too cute with a name choice so that your consulting business sounds amateurish. If your name is Mark Fish, for example, "Fish Food for Thought" might be a great name for an aquarium business, but not for a consulting business. You want to be taken seriously.

The goal is to make it easy for your clients to select you by name the first time and to remember you by name forever after. You will build up name recognition the longer you consult. Therefore, select something that you will be able to live with for a long time. You may also want to think about the graphics that could support your name. Although it took the marketing agency nine months to convince me to use waves with my corporate name, "ebb," it has proven to be the right choice. Clients relate the visual to the name.

You may also want to consider how you intend to brand your business. Will you be a loud and in-their-face kind of consultant? Or will you be formal and strong? Or maybe fun and creative? You may think it is a bit early to consider this now, but your corporate name will help tell your story and brand your services. The name is an important aspect of marketing your services.

Think also about the images that come to mind with the names you have chosen. How might they appear on all types of media you may choose in the future: stationery, business cards, Web site, maybe even a billboard.

If your business name is anything besides your own, you are required to register it with the secretary of state's office in the state where you intend to do business. In addition, if you use any name in addition to the one you've chosen, you must file a Certificate of Trade Name or a "doing business as" (DBA) certificate. For example,

Quick ▶ TIP

If you are having difficulty deciding on a name or even thinking of some creative possibilities that follow the listed guidelines, go to www. namingtoolbox.com or www.entrepreneurs.about.com The first is software that will help you generate possible names. The second is a Web site that describes a process for naming a business. Once you get to the Web site, click on "Starting a Business." The Web site also offers other services to entrepreneurs. Once you have selected a couple of possible names, use your favorite search engine to conduct a quick check to determine if the name is being used in any other way.

your corporation may be Greene Ventures, Inc., and you may name your consulting practice Corporate Computer Consulting. This practice allows you to do business in states where someone else is already known as Green Ventures, Inc. In addition, this practice allows you to incorporate once and have flexibility for various new start-ups. Contact your local city or state officials for more information.

And if you wish to trademark your name, you will need your attorney's assistance.

List eight possible names here for your business. Then try them out on colleagues to get feedback.

1.

2.

3.

4.

5.

6.

7.

8.

Find the Best Accountant and Attorney

You will need to find an accountant and an attorney immediately. You may be thinking that it is too early for an accountant—you haven't made any money yet! An accountant is necessary at this time to provide good advice for the many decisions you will be making. An attorney will also get you started on the right foot and let you know what records you should keep.

You will find a good accountant the same way you find good restaurants, dry cleaners, and barbers: networking. Ask other businesspeople, especially other consultants, whom they use. Identify the qualities you are looking for so that you can describe your ideal accountant. In the best case, you will find someone who has experience with small consulting start-ups.

Interview several accountants before you select the one with whom you will work. This is one of the most important relationships in your business. You will work with your accountant at least once a month.

What are you looking for in an accountant?

- Keeps you informed of new tax laws?
- Keeps you informed of retirement law changes?
- Challenges you?
- Takes risks or is risk averse?

What services do you want your accountant to provide?

- Tax preparation?
- Monthly record keeping?
- Monthly statement generation?
- Payroll services?

When I found a great accountant, I asked her to recommend an attorney. You can do the same, and with a little luck the person will meet your needs. You will experience more value if your accountant and your attorney already collaborate on other business.

Even with a recommendation from your accountant, spend time interviewing the attorney. You want to feel comfortable that the person will meet your needs. You might ask these questions in your interview:

- What experience have you had with consulting firms?
- How have you worked with my accountant in the past?
- How can we best work together?
- How do you charge for the work you do: flat fee or hourly rate?
- Can you provide some examples of flat fee rates for services I might use?
- If you charge an hourly rate, what is that rate?
- What determines whether someone else in the firm will work with me?
- Do different attorneys in the firm bill at different rates?
- What other costs are involved?
- How can you be reached in times of emergency (through office staff or at home)?

After your interview, reflect on these questions:

- How comfortable did you feel with the attorney?
- Was the attorney interested in you?
- Did you understand everything the attorney told you?
- Did the attorney use words you understood and define those you didn't?
- Did the attorney's answers meet your needs?
- Do you feel that this attorney will have your best interests in mind?
- Will you feel comfortable calling the attorney with questions?

After you have decided on an accountant and an attorney, the first thing they will do for you is to help you decide on the best business structure for your consulting business.

Find an Accountant and Attorney

Identify three possible accountants or attorneys (or both) now. Be sure to ask your network for suggestions.

Accountants

1.

2.

3.

Attorneys

1.

2.

3.

Begin to schedule interviews with these people over the next couple of weeks.

Determine Your Business Structure

The next step is to determine the best business structure for your situation. Once you have found an accountant and an attorney, take your plans to them, and ask for their advice. Determining a business structure may be confusing; however, in the United States, there are basically only five types:

- Sole proprietorships
- Partnerships
- Corporations (C and S)
- Limited liability companies
- Limited liability partnerships

If you are forming your consulting business outside the United States, seek advice from someone who understands the laws regarding business structures in that country. Also, be aware that laws are different from state to state. If you plan to do business outside your state, be sure to discuss this with your accountant and attorney.

Sole Proprietorship

A sole proprietorship is the simplest business structure. It is not a separate legal entity from the owner, and usually your social security number serves as your company's federal taxpayer identification number. There is no registration requirement other than an assumed name filing if you want to do business in another state or under a different name.

Partnerships

Partnerships are formed when two or more people form a business entity. Each general partner has an equal voice in managing the business, which is identified by a federal employer identification number (FEIN). The traditional partnership is known as a *general partnership*. A *limited partnership* has limited partners in addition to the general partners. Limited partners share in the profit and loss, have limited rights to managing the business, and have limited liability.

Corporations

Corporations can be formed as C corporations or as Subchapter-S corporations. All corporations are separate and distinct legal entities, and ownership interests can be transferred. To form a corporation, you must file articles of incorporation, receive a charter issued by a state, create bylaws, and fulfill other state requirements. Subchapter-S corporations have the distinct advantage of not being double-taxed as a C corporation is. This means the owners pay taxes as a corporation and again as individuals.

Limited Liability Structures

Limited liability companies (LLCs) and limited liability partnerships (LLPs) have a corporate look but qualify for other partnership or corporate tax status. As more relaxed entities, they combine limited liability protection without all the corporate formalities. They represent a newer structure, so some attorneys and accountants are just becoming comfortable with them.

The Comparison of Basic Business Entities chart provides you with a comparison of characteristics of these business structures. Examine it before visiting your accountant or attorney.

The Business Structure That's Best for You

Your attorney and accountant will help you determine the business structure that's best for you. Complete the Business Entity Selection Worksheet here, and take your responses to them. The answers to these questions will also prepare you to develop your business plan in Chapter Five. As you and your professionals compare the different business structures, consider these issues:

- Cost of forming
- Process for filing
- Cost to maintain and operate the entity
- Liability risks
- Formalities to operate, such as requirements to hold annual meetings or submit meeting minutes to the state in which you incorporate
- Ability to transfer ownership

Comparison of Basic Business Entities

Entity	Owner Liability	Participation in Management	Ownership	Formation Requirements	Name
Sole Proprietor	No limits.	No restrictions.	One.	None. File assumed name if doing business in another state or under different name.	No special requirements.
General Partnership	No limits.	No restrictions.	At least two partners.	Partnership agreement (may be oral) and file assumed name certificate.	No special requirements.
Limited Partnership	No limits for general partners. Limited for limited partners.	Restrictions for limited partners.	At least one general partner and one limited partner.	Partnership agreement (may be oral) and file certificate with Secretary of State.	Must have "Limited Partnership," "Ltd.," "Limited," or "L.P." in title.
Limited Liability Company	All members have limited liability for company debts.	No restrictions. ("Managing" members make decisions.)	One or more members. (Some states may require at least two members.)	File Articles of Organization and adopt regulations.	Must have "Limited Liability Company," "LLC," or "LC" in title. ("Limited" and "Company" may be abbreviated.)

Comparison of Basic Business Entities *Cont'd*

Entity	Owner Liability	Participation in Management	Ownership	Formation Requirements	Name
S Corporation	Limited liability for all shareholders.	No restrictions. (Shareholders elect directors to make decisions. Directors appoint officers for daily decisions.)	One to seventy-five shareholders.	File Articles of Incorporation, adopt bylaws, and file "S" election tax form with IRS.	Must have "Corporation," "Incorporated," "Company," or abbreviation of one of these in title.
C Corporation	Limited liability for all shareholders.	No restrictions. (Shareholders elect directors to make decisions. Directors appoint officers for daily decisions.)	One or more shareholders.	File Articles of Incorporation and adopt bylaws.	Must have some form of "Corporation," "Incorporated," "Company," or abbreviation of one of these in title.

Source: Biech & Swindling, *The Consultant's Legal Guide*, 2000.

- Length of time you expect your business to exist
- Amount of privacy you require

Business Entity Selection Worksheet

Ask yourself these questions as you decide on the best business entity for you. Review the answers with your attorney and accountant to help make your structure decisions.

What type of business are you creating?

What services and/or products will you offer?

How will you distribute those services and/or products?

Where will the business operations be located?

Who will own this business?

How much of the business will each person own?

Who will manage the business, and what role will each person play?

What is your financial plan?

How much capital will you require? When? In what form?

What are your start-up costs?

What are your income projections?

How will profits and losses be allocated?

What are the financial resources of the owners?

What are the assets of the business?

What action will you take if you are not meeting your financial goals?

Who is your competition?

What is your marketing strategy?

Where is your customer base located?

How long do you plan to be in business?

Do you plan to sell the business someday?

Will you want to sell part of the business to raise money? (Stock or membership interest?)

Do you plan to transfer the business to a family member?

Do you have any estate planning issues regarding the business?

Are there any special tax issues regarding your type of business?

Are there any special laws or regulatory constraints on your type of business or on the owners?

What is your potential exposure to risks and liabilities?

What is your potential risk in addition to the equity invested in the business?

How will you keep track of the legal requirements or formalities of your business entity?

What happens on death, disability, retirement, or departure of a principal?

Finalize Your Decision About Structure

The business structure for _____ (name) will be _____.
The key reasons are:

Explore Your Banking and Insurance Needs

A banker and good insurance providers will also be important members of your business team.

Bank on Good Advice

Establish a separate bank account for your business from the start. Using your personal checking account may seem easier, but for good record keeping, it is wise to separate the accounts. Besides, the law requires it of partnerships and corporations. You will also be required to file a Schedule C with your income tax return, and a separate bank account makes this easier. Commingled business and personal funds may raise tax issues and liability issues for you later. Don't take a chance. Keep personal finances and business finances separate. Some people use separate banks to avoid confusion or errors.

Your banking needs may not seem critical initially, but you will find that a good banker can become a close and valuable partner. How do you select one? Ask your accountant and your attorney for recommendations. If the members of your support team work together, it will often be more helpful to you. You can also ask other businesspeople for suggestions.

Be certain that each bank is financially sound, follows established commercial banking practices, and has a good customer service reputation. Then interview each potential banker about the bank's services and methods of operation. You might begin with these questions:

- Is the bank federally insured?
- Does it offer the services you need today:

- Loans in the amount you anticipate?

- Checking accounts?

- Money market accounts?

- Certificate of deposit accounts?

- Advisory services?

- Safe-deposit box?

- Wire transfer?

- Electronic banking?

- Direct deposit?

- Night drop?

- Trust services?

- IRA or 401k?

- How experienced is management?

- What experience have they had with consulting firms?

- If you plan to work internationally, can the bank handle foreign currencies?

- Can the bank help you set up payroll deductions for IRAs?

- What kind of fees will you pay for your checking account? Is it free with a minimum balance?

- How soon will you need to order checks? How much will they cost?

- Can you easily bank by computer?

- How can you access your account information?

- Is ATM access readily available?

- How do you qualify for a revolving line of credit and for what amount?

- What business advice does the bank provide regularly and in what format, such as in brochures, by phone, or through seminars?

- What networking capabilities does the bank have? Can it put you in touch with suppliers, potential clients, or other business owners?

- How well did you connect with the people you interviewed? How comfortable will you be discussing your financial needs with them in the future?

- What needs does the bank think you might anticipate in the future that you did not ask about?

Be sure to discuss possible financing for your consulting business. The estimates you prepared of personal income and expenses in Chapter Two should give you an idea of when you might need financing. It's probably best to wait to request specific financing until you have completed your business plan in Chapter Five and your transition plan in Chapter Six. Nevertheless, it's good to test the waters with your bank now. How open and receptive do the people you are consulting with seem about financing, and what options do they suggest?

Insure Your Success

Insurance is a way to transfer some of the risk to another entity. For a consultant starting out, several types of insurance coverage are essential, and others might be nice to have. A word of caution: Don't skimp on insurance. It is worth the peace of mind to be well covered.

Review all of your insurance needs with an agent you can trust. This does not mean, however, that you should not shop around for the best coverage at the lowest price. I recently purchased a commercial building and wanted to use the insurance agent I already have because we had built a relationship. When I went out for bids on the new property, I was able to get more coverage for almost six hundred dollars less with another reputable agency. I took the figure back to my agent, who just shook her head and said she could not match it. I still asked her to look over the new policy and to reassure me that the company was reputable.

If you have an insurance agent, start there, though recognize that all agents do not cover all insurance needs. If you don't currently have an insurance agent, interview potential insurance agents, and consider these questions:

- How many kinds of insurance do you represent?

- How many insurance companies do you represent?

- What kinds of policies have you written for consultants?

- What references can you provide from other consultants?

- What insurance coverage do you think I need?

- What are the features of the policies you recommend?

- What is the rating for the insurance companies you propose to handle my needs?

What kind of insurance might you need? Most employees take for granted the insurance provided to them by their employers: health, life, disability, business liability, and others. As you move to self-employed status, you are probably focused on health insurance for yourself and your family. While health insurance is certainly critical, don't forget about other essential insurance. Consider coverage for some or all of these kinds of insurance:

- *Health.* If you work for a company of twenty or more employees, you qualify for COBRA (Consolidated Omnibus Budget Reconciliation Act) coverage, which provides you the opportunity to continue with the company's group health insurance plan for eighteen months after leaving the company. You will pay the premiums yourself, but it is usually less expensive than the individual policy you will eventually use. Use this temporarily, and have your permanent insurance in place six to eight weeks before COBRA expires. You have these options for permanent health insurance: your professional association may offer group plans or discounts; if your spouse works, you might be added to your spouse's policy; or you can obtain individual policies through agencies.
- *Disability.* These benefits are paid if you cannot work. Although many people often overlook this insurance, as a self-employed consultant, you cannot afford to ignore disability insurance.
- *Casualty.* Sometimes called property insurance, it covers damage, destruction, or theft of property.
- *Liability.* This coverage protects you if someone is hurt on your property. You should consider coverage of at least $5 million.
- *Professional liability.* This protects you from claims by clients you caused injury or harm to (including financial loss) due to mistakes in the service you provided. Although it is expensive and difficult to locate (check to see which insurance companies offer this type of service), you should at least consider it. Consultants

can buy protection for errors and omissions (E&O), a type of professional liability, through a professional or trade association. For example, the International Computer Consultants Association offers this coverage to its members.

● *Workers' compensation.* This is regulated and standardized by state governments, and you will most likely purchase it from a broker. As a sole proprietor, you may exclude yourself from this coverage, but you are responsible for coverage for all employees and sometimes subcontractors you may employ.

There is other coverage you might consider as well: business interruption, crime, rent, group health, retirement income, and key-man insurance. It is best to discuss your requirements with your insurance agent.

Use the following list to discuss your insurance needs with an insurance agent or broker. Even if you have coverage, you will want to explain your intentions for consulting. For example, if you intend to work from your home and you have a home owner's policy, it may not cover injuries to someone visiting for business purposes or the full value of business equipment you have in your home. Your auto insurance may not cover you if you use your car for business purposes.

My Business Insurance Needs

Type of Insurance	Recommended Coverage and Limits	Cost
Automobile		
Business interruption		
Casualty		
Crime		
Disability		
Error and omissions		
Health		

Liability

Professional liability

Rent

Workers' compensation

Other

Quick  TIP

Want to read more about insurance for small businesses? Check the Insurance Information Institute's Web site for insuring a small business at www. iii.org/smallbusiness/intro/, where you will find an excellent glossary and other information about all the various insurances to consider.

Check Local Zoning Laws, Licenses, and Taxes

Your accountant and attorney will probably remind you of your obligations as a business owner, but it is still your responsibility to ensure that you do everything required.

Zoning laws are usually regulated by the municipality in which you intend to operate. If you are considering an office in your home, check out pertinent zoning laws. Local zoning restrictions might prevent you from having employees, posting signs, or operating certain types of businesses from your home.

Every city is different; therefore, call about the zoning ordinances that cover your situation. Unfortunately, the name of the office will be different in every city as well. It may be called the zoning board, building code, code compliance, or something else. A few calls should eventually get you to the right person. Once that happens, ask for the specific zoning ordinances that cover your situation. If the person says there is no problem, keep a record of your discussion and the name of the person who provided this information.

If there is a restriction that prevents you from having a consulting practice in your home, you can always ask for a variance—an alteration that grants a change for one person. For example, if you are planning to hire a part-time clerical person and the zoning laws prohibit you from employing nonfamily members in your home, you could file a formal application for a variance with your local government. Be sure to check on all the procedures before you make your request:

- Where do you make your application?

- Do you need your neighbors' approval?

- Do you need their approval in writing?

- Do you need to attend the board meeting in person?

- Do you need architectural drawings?

Follow the procedures. Not doing so may result in a delay, and in some municipalities, the zoning board may meet as infrequently as every six months.

During the same time you are checking on zoning laws, determine whether your city or state requires you to have a business license for your consulting practice.

And finally, check on taxes. Some large cities require that you pay a city tax on your gross income. It is often quite small—as little as 0.5 percent. In some cases, if you do business in two cities and one does not charge a city tax, the second one might lay claim to all your work. Your accountant will assist you with these questions and calculate how much tax you owe.

File Legal Documentation

Once you've determined the best structure for your business, file documentation to legally register it. Your attorney will assist you with filing the documentation required.

Also request your federal employer identification number (EIN). You will need this number—if you have chosen anything except a sole proprietorship—to file tax returns, open a business bank account, deposit employment taxes (if you have employees), and establish a company retirement plan.

To obtain your EIN, file IRS Form SS-4. The form looks formidable, but it asks only eighteen questions, and you can answer all of them by this point. If you forget to do this now and later urgently need the number (for example, you want to open a checking account), it is possible to have a number assigned over the telephone. Simply follow the instructions printed on the form.

You may also need a state employer identification number. Check with your state's Department of Revenue (or Taxation) and Department of Labor for the requirements. If you live outside the United States, you will need to contact your appropriate government agencies.

Once you've worked through all the activities in this chapter, your consulting business should feel closer to reality. Putting your business plan together in the next chapter will firm up that reality even more.

Quick Start ACTION

Your First To-Do List

Okay. You've read through (and probably written in) this book for four chapters. It is time you took some action—that is, if you haven't already! In Chapter Five, you will begin to write a business plan. It will be helpful if you have completed several tasks prior to that time. Here's the beginning of your first to-do list. If you have already completed items on the list, good for you! Check them off. It is time to turn your thinking, planning, and considering into action. Note that the worksheets in the first four chapters help you complete the actions. Be sure to add others that are unique to your needs.

My To-Do List

❏   Meet with a consultant.

❏   Assess my skills.

❏   Identify the focus of my consulting practice.

❏   Talk to my family about what I am thinking.

❏   Meet with several colleagues to get their thoughts.

❏   Complete my budget figures.

❏   Determine my financial requirements (budget) and pricing structure.

❏   Identify my start-up costs.

❏   Finalize what I intend to charge clients.

❏   Name my business.

❏   Select and meet with an accountant.

❏   Determine my business structure.

❏   Select a banker, attorney, and insurance agent.

❏   Determine my insurance needs.

❏   Arrange for financing (or set aside capital for a worst case-scenario).

❏   File documentation to legally register my business.

❏   Check on zoning laws, licenses, and taxes.

❏   Select a location.

Quick Start LISTS

Actions I Will Take

Ideas I Have

Questions I Have

Your Business Plan

In this chapter you will

- Develop your business plan
- Determine how you will use your business plan

Are Business Plans Really Necessary?

This chapter is about planning: developing a business plan and then determining how you will implement that plan. A business plan is a document that describes your consulting business and where you want it to go in the future. Many new consultants are impatient to get started with the real work of consulting, so planning at this time may seem to be a waste of time when there is so much else to do. Planning may seem less critical than earning money when there is no income yet. Planning may not seem very action oriented and, quite frankly, you may find it boring! Fewer than half of all businesses take the time to write a business plan.

Nevertheless, a business plan is a critical document. Let's remind ourselves of the value of writing a business plan from the perspective of both the process and the result:

The Process

- Encourages you to think strategically
- Forces you to face difficult issues and concerns

- Provides you with a realistic view of actions that require your attention

- Compels you to think about all key aspects of the business (marketing, financial, product or service)

- Stimulates new ideas

- Creates time for you to organize all of your ideas in one place

The Result

- Delineates the strengths and weaknesses of your plan

- Communicates your vision and expectations for the future

- Provides a presentation package to raise money

- Provides a guide for making decisions about the business

- Becomes a tool for measuring progress

- Creates a road map for the future

- Serves as a reference document

Still not convinced that writing a business plan is a necessity? Perhaps you should identify why you are avoiding the task. Answer the following questions to help you understand your underlying reluctance. Do not read the next section until you complete this activity. This activity will reveal much about you if you complete it without reading ahead. (If you are already sold on the idea of writing a business plan, you may skip the questions, go on to the next section, and begin to write your business plan.)

1. How do you feel about investing time in writing a business plan? How urgent do you think writing the business plan is compared to the other things you need to do as you set up your consulting business?

2. How do you feel about sharing your business plan with others? How about sharing it with friends?

3. How prepared are you to write a business plan? How knowledgeable are you about business plans in general?

4. How do you rate your writing skills? What concerns do you have related to your ability to write a business plan?

5. How thorough is your knowledge of consulting and your potential customers?

6. How confident are you that you will be 100 percent successful in the consulting field?

Evaluating Your Responses

Although the questions were related specifically to writing your business plan, your answers divulge much about you, such as how you approach tasks and where you may stumble as an entrepreneur. Here is how to evaluate your responses:

1. How did you respond about the time investment?   If you responded that you thought it would be a waste of time, perhaps you do not appreciate the value of planning and how much time can actually be saved (or gained) by good planning. You may have responded that you think it's a good use of time, but you just don't have time now. The question is, If you don't have time now, when will you?

What might this answer say about you as an entrepreneur? Planning is critical to starting any business. Although some businesses fail due to a lack of financing or poor management, most actually fail due to inadequate planning. Don't fall into that trap. In addition, time will always be an issue for you. Once you begin consulting, you will find that you will often have more to do than time to do it. For example, you will find it almost impossible to find time to market when you're engrossed with a huge project. Yet you must market, even though you are too busy to market, or you may not have work when you've completed the project you are working on now. As a consultant you will always be juggling many balls, and many of those balls will be urgent. You will need to find the time to do it all—and do it all with quality. You will find that there is always more to do than you think you will have time to complete.

Do you truly appreciate the value of planning? Are you always able to find time to complete critical events? How well do you juggle numerous tasks at one time?

2. How do you feel about sharing your business plan with others? One of the reasons for developing a business plan is to raise capital for your business, so of course you want to be comfortable discussing it with potential investors. But what about sharing it with family and friends? How appreciative will you be of their critiques? How objective can you be about suggestions that might change your plans? Some time ago, our company designed an off-the-shelf package for teaching process improvement skills. The kit, Process Tamer, is a proven process, was created using all the best adult learning theory, and was designed using only the highest-quality components. Because the price point was over a thousand dollars, a publisher friend, Dick Roe, advised against moving forward. He suggested we were throwing away $100,000—the development cost. I didn't listen. He was right, and it was one of the costliest lessons of my consulting career. Are there other reasons you do not want to share your ideas? Are you worried about what others might say if you do not meet your goals? If you are reluctant to share your business plan because you do not want to hear the feedback, you may be missing valuable opportunities to hone your plan.

What might this say about you as an entrepreneur? Successful entrepreneurs must be receptive to others' comments. As a consultant, you must always be open to ideas and information. Remember that you are selling yourself. Therefore, you must make yourself more valuable. Feedback—whether supportive or critical—will make you more valuable. Even if you do not believe that the feedback is correct, the perception is there for a reason. Dig deeper, and learn more. Try to treat the information objectively. Of course, this isn't easy, but good consultants are thick-skinned. You must be prepared to receive feedback, hear bad consultant jokes, and even be called names, such as beltway bandit or con man. You must consider what you hear, and be objective about what you might do with the information. You'll be better for it.

Are you comfortable discussing your plans with others? How open are you to hearing negative feedback? How objective can you be to others' ideas? Are you able to discern valuable feedback from feedback that will not be helpful? Are you able to consider all ideas at their face value or for what might be behind them?

3. How did you respond about being prepared and knowledgeable about writing business plans? Does your response indicate a reluctance to begin writing because you do not know how to write a business plan or because you do not have experience in developing one? If so, what have you done to address this gap? As a consultant, you will find yourself in many situations in which you will not know exactly what to do. Lucky (and rare) is the consultant who walks into every project knowing exactly what needs to be accomplished. If you do not feel confident about writing your business plan because you've never done one before, you are experiencing something that is consistent with consulting: starting something for which you do not know the answer.

What might this say about you as an entrepreneur? Entrepreneurs do not have all the answers to everything, but they do know how to find the answers. And when they don't know how to find the answer, they just begin. Consultants often need to be the epitome of Nike's "just do it." Consultants rarely have the luxury of giving up. Consultants are persistent.

How do you respond when you hit a dead end? Are you willing to conduct research or use networking to resolve problems? Are you able to just begin and have faith that you will reach solutions?

4. How did you respond about your ability to write? Writing is a basic form of communication with which all consultants must feel comfortable. I listed it in Chapter One as one of the skills required of a consultant. You will most likely need to write proposals, reports, letters, marketing materials, and many other documents. Your writing will project an image of you as a consultant. If you are not confident in your writing ability, you may wish to consider hiring someone to edit and proof your work. You may also want to register for a class at your local college or technical school.

What might this say about you as an entrepreneur? Recognizing a weakness and admitting it are critical for success. The successful entrepreneur will find a way to overcome a weakness. As a consultant, you may not possess all the skills required for success. But if you have identified your weaknesses and determined how you will compensate, you are ahead of the game. You have at least two choices. First, you may learn the information or acquire the skills. Second, you may tap into someone else who has the knowledge or skill, for example, by hiring someone, working with a partner or adviser, identifying support contractors, or using your own consultant.

What weaknesses or skill and knowledge gaps do you have as a consultant? What plans do you have to overcome them?

5. How knowledgeable are you about the profession of consulting and your customers? It's going to be difficult to write a business plan without this information.

You may have a general idea of how you intend to consult, but specifics are necessary. If your response suggests that you still need to learn more, you may find that you will need to conduct more research, gather more data, and learn more before proceeding with your plans. Have you completed the step in Chapter One in which you were to interview a consultant? That is the very least that you should do. To gain more knowledge, you may want to join a professional organization such as the American Society for Training and Development, the Association of Management Consulting, the Institute of Management Consultants, or one that specializes in your unique area such as the Independent Computer Consultants Association or the American Society of Consulting Arborists. You may also want to interview potential clients whom you locate through your network.

What might this say about you as an entrepreneur? The most successful entrepreneurs have both depth and breadth of knowledge about their chosen field. As a consultant, you will want to commit yourself to learning everything you can about the profession and about your potential customers.

What do you still need to know about the profession of consulting? What organizations should you join? What books and journals should you read? How can you learn more about your customers?

6. How did you answer the confidence question? How confidently did you answer this question? If you have any self-doubts or fear of failure, a plan can do a great deal to eliminate those concerns. A well-done business plan will describe the concerns and provide the answers. Does your response suggest that you might fail at writing a business plan? In order to sleep at night, you need confidence that you can accomplish anything you set your mind to do.

What might this say about you as an entrepreneur? Entrepreneurs, especially consultants, must be passionate about what they do. Successful entrepreneurs are absolutely and unequivocally certain of success. I remember making the decision to move into the consulting field. As I played with the numbers—various formulas of how much work I expected, what kind of work I could do, and how much I thought clients might pay—I remember thinking, "I can't not succeed!" Passion about your success must start with you. If you don't believe in you, who will? Henry Ford said, "If you believe you can or cannot, you will prove yourself correct." You must believe that you hold the destiny of your business in your hands. You must feel confident of your success.

How confident are you that you will succeed as a consultant? Do you believe that you will achieve all of your goals? Are you passionate about being a consultant? Do you believe in your own success? Will you be able to sell yourself with confidence?

The point of the exercise above was twofold: to identify what might be holding you back from writing a business plan and, more important, to find out what your excuses for not getting on with the business plan suggest about your consulting weaknesses. If any of the comments ring true for you, return to Chapter One to review your self-assessments. Pay particular attention to your responses to "Are You a Match for the Profession?" on page 9 and the "Entrepreneur Attitude Survey" on page 13. Now that you have a specific task to complete—writing your business plan—compare your responses in Chapter One against how you approached the task. Then develop your personal improvement plan here.

1. Would you change anything about your self-assessment? If yes, what?

2. What might you do to gain the experience, skills, knowledge, and aptitude for becoming a consultant?

3. How might you use other individuals to contribute or fill in what you might be missing?

When you are satisfied that you are ready to move on, begin to complete your business plan in the next section.

Write Your Plan

A business plan is generally five to ten pages, plus several additional supporting documents. The plan may have several iterations and revisions. You may begin to write it and find that you need to conduct more research. You may also find that you haven't thought through all of your ideas as thoroughly as you need and must revise your earlier business design. Don't get discouraged. It is far better to discover these things now than later.

In *The Business of Consulting,* second edition, I present a business plan template that you can download from the CD. The plan you are about to prepare matches that template in design and detail. If you anticipate borrowing money to start your business, this plan provides the kind of detail required to attract investors. Use this book to jot down your ideas first. It will help you see where you will need to gather more information. You may not be able to answer all the questions presented, and that's okay, but you should make a concerted effort to answer most of them. Once you've captured your notes here, go to your computer and begin to write the narrative.

Your business plan has these sections: a cover page, table of contents, business description, market analysis, competitive analysis, marketing plan, management plan, financial plan, and appendixes that contain financial documentation and supporting documents.

Quick •••••••••••••••••••••• ▶ **TIP**

Go to the Internet or call several publicly owned companies to obtain copies of their annual reports. Although you will not write anything nearly as elaborate as these publications, they will provide you with inspiration, examples of mission statements, and business language that is used.

Cover Page

The cover is the first page that your readers see, and it sets the tone for the rest of the business plan. First impressions are important, so present your best image. A cover page tells the reader that you take this business plan seriously and provides all the information necessary for someone to get in touch with you. The cover also includes a date so that you know which edition of the plan you are using. Fill in your information on the following sample page. For your actual cover page, consider adding some line graphics as shown here or color. Add your logo if you have one.

A Business Plan

for

[company name & logo]

ebb associates inc

[Date]

Owner:
Address:
Telephone:
E-mail:
Web site:

Table of Contents

The table of contents provides another opportunity for you to impress your business plan reader by showing your organizational skills. The following example gives the suggested sections for a business plan.

Table of Contents

Business Description
Market Analysis
Competitive Analysis
Marketing Plan
Management Plan
Financial Plan
Appendices
      Financial Statements
      (list each)
      Supporting Documents
      (list each)

Business Description

This will most likely be the longest and the most important section of your business plan. Begin it with an introduction that states the purpose of the business plan. Follow this with a description of your consulting business. You may divide the description into your plans for the business, the work you will conduct, and the business's demographics. Use the following questions to guide you:

- Introduction
  - What is the purpose of the business plan?
- Your plans for the business
  - What is the mission, vision, and/or purpose of your consulting business?
  - What are your goals for the business? (Your goals should be specific, measurable, and time bound.)

- The work

  - What specific activities does the business do to raise revenue?

  - What services or products will it provide?

  - Why do you believe your business will succeed?

  - What relevant experience do you bring to the business of consulting?

- Demographics

  - What is the name of the business? The address? Telephone and fax numbers? What is the e-mail address? What is the URL for the Web site?

  - Who is (are) the owner(s)?

  - What's the business structure? If it is incorporated, where?

  - What information is important about the start of this business? For example, is it a new business or an expansion of an existing business? What was the start-up date?

Market Analysis

The market analysis will be most beneficial for financial support if you can quote statistics about consulting, your consulting specialty, or the industry you have chosen. You may find some of these data in industry journals or on the Internet. *Training* magazine and the American Society for Training and Development conduct research each year that might provide data for some consultants. Kennedy Publishing and *Consulting* magazine are other good sources.

Address these questions in the analysis:

- What industry or industries are you targeting?

- Are you in a stable, growing, or declining industry?

- What is occurring now or is expected to occur in the future that will affect your business either negatively or positively?

- Who are your current customers?

- Who are your potential customers?

- What are the demographics of your current and potential client base?

- What is the size of your potential market? What percentage of the market do you expect to penetrate?

- What's the estimated total market in dollar value?

Quick ▶ **TIP**

Kennedy Publishing is a consulting research firm that provides data for market analysis during this stage of your business and then keeps you abreast of what's happening in the industry. The Web site is www.Kennedyinformation.com. *Consulting* magazine can be found at www.consultingmag.com.

Competitive Analysis

This section examines the competition you expect to face. It should answer these questions:

- Who is your competition?

- How would you describe your competition in the geographical and specialty areas you have targeted?

- How do your consulting products or services differ from those of your competitors?

- How do your competitors' pricing structures compare to yours?

- What experience do your competitors have?

- How strong is the name recognition of each of your competitors?

- What share of the market do these targeted competitors have?

- Is your competitors' business increasing, decreasing, or remaining steady?

- Why would someone buy from a competitor instead of you?

- How do your competitors market themselves?

- What are your comparative strengths and weaknesses in sales or marketing?

- What differentiates you from your competitors?

Quick ················▶ **TIP**

Develop your Top Ten list of reasons that clients would hire you. This list will help you bridge the step from competitive analysis to your marketing plan.

Marketing Plan

You can use the following questions to develop a simple marketing plan:

- Describe your market niche in detail:

  - What size company will you serve?

  - What specific geographical area will you serve?

  - What kinds of organizations will you serve?

  - Will you serve special situations, such as start-ups or mergers?

- What are your pricing strategy and structure? How do they differ from those of your competitors?

- What marketing tactics will you pursue? What advertising? What promotion?

- How will you implement tactics throughout the year?

- What expertise will you use to develop your marketing plan?

  You will develop a more in-depth marketing plan in Chapter Nine.

Management Plan

Answer these questions about how you intend to manage your consulting business:

- Who are the key players in your business? What are their duties, compensation, and benefits?

- If you are the sole employee, how will you manage all that needs to be completed? What is your starting salary?

- What resources are available if you need assistance?

- When do you expect to hire additional personnel—if ever?

- What experience do you bring to the business in marketing, sales, managing a business, and other supporting roles?

- What is your education level?

- What professional support will you use, such as an attorney, accountant, or banker?

- What banking services will you use, and where? What process will you use to establish credit?

Financial Plan

Use these questions to write the narrative, and support your narrative with financial statements in the appendix:

- What assumptions are you making as a basis of the plan, such as market health, start-up date, gross profit margin, required overhead, payroll, and other expenses?

- What expenditures will you require for start-up?

- What are your cash flow projections for each month of your first year?

- What are your three-year cash flow projections?

- Where do you expect to find financing and under what terms? How will the money be used—for example, for overhead, supplies, marketing?

- Do you have a line of credit? How much is it?
- What is your personal net worth as displayed in a financial statement?

Appendices

The appendices contain documents that support your narrative. They may be divided into two sections or more. You may wish to include those listed here.

Financial Documentation

- Start-up expenses
- Budget
- First-year cash flow projections
- Three-year projections
- Personal financial statement
- If you are already operating, an income statement from the past year

Supporting Documents

- Testimonials from satisfied clients
- References
- Demographic information
- Your résumé
- Biographical sketches of your accountant, attorney, and others
- Industry data or demographics

Printing Your Business Plan

Once you've completed your plan, have it edited and proofread. You may wish to give it to several people—some who know the consulting business well, others who can edit for typos, spelling, and grammatical errors. Make the corrections, and print out a clean copy of your business plan on high-quality paper. You may wish to put it in a clear-front document binder. If you have pocket folders that you are using for your business, you may wish to tuck the plan inside as a finished product (and add a brochure and a business card if you have them).

Plan to Use Your Business Plan

Whatever you do with the plan, do not put it on a shelf. It should become a working document that you refer to regularly.

Keep the plan handy, and use it to help you make decisions. Check your business progress against the plan at least quarterly to keep yourself focused. And if something is not working, change your direction. "Staying focused" does not mean staying the course even when something is not working. Modify your strategies if they are not as effective as you originally envisioned. Keep your long-term vision in mind, and continue to move in that direction.

Consider the following to ensure that your business plan serves its purpose:

- Check the data from which you are operating at least twice each year to ensure they are still current.

- Read the *Wall Street Journal* daily to be knowledgeable about the industries in which you work.

- Subscribe to the *Harvard Business Review, Fortune* magazine, and *Fast Company* magazine (at least) to stay on top of business and management trends.

- Read books written by leaders you respect to inspire new ideas for your consulting business.

- Attend conferences that focus on improving your skills and knowledge in the areas you have designated as needing improvement.

- Network with other consultants.

- Learn as much as you can from customers about their existing needs, but also become adept at predicting their needs.

- Never hesitate to pick up the telephone and call someone in your networking sphere to discuss something in your plan that doesn't seem to be working.

Use all of the information from these suggestions to update your business plan and ensure that you are focused on an appropriate vision.

Plan a Review

After you complete your business plan and before you leave this chapter, schedule a date with yourself (write it in your calendar or enter it into your electronic planner) to review your business plan. Schedule that date for six to twelve weeks out, depending on where you are in the process of establishing your consulting business. If you're just starting, do this in six weeks; if you have been consulting for some time, you could wait as long as twelve weeks. You decide what seems appropriate to you.

Alternatively, you may wish to consider bringing together a small group of advisers to provide an analysis of your progress. Perhaps start with you accountant (or maybe your banker and attorney depending on your relationship with them) and several colleagues whose opinions you value. Three or four people will be enough. They can serve as a quasi-board of directors for you. Send them your business plan now, and ask for their thoughts. In addition, ask them if they would be willing to meet with you in four to six months for a review of your progress. The results will be well worth your effort.

Quick Start LISTS

Actions I Will Take

Ideas I Have

Questions I Have

Make the Switch Painlessly

In this chapter you will

- Identify opportunities to gain consulting experience before leaving your job
- Determine your transition plan

Gain Consulting Experience Before Leaving Your Job

You can gain consulting experience before you leave the safety net of your full-time job. You should identify several opportunities to get experience prior to leaving your job. For example, perhaps you can:

- Facilitate a weekend retreat for a local volunteer group

- Conduct a team-building session for a civic organization

- Offer your services on a freelance basis to a subsidiary or another firm in your company's business group.

- Design new software for a local school system
- Teach a class at your community college

How could you gain experience in your chosen consulting area before you leave your job?

Getting Started

This book has focused on starting your own consulting business. There are any number of ways to enter the field:

As an employee. Many employment opportunities exist for you, from the small consulting firms in your city that have more work than they can handle to one of the large national consulting firms. A local company can provide you with a vast variety of projects, and you are likely to find yourself in charge of a project relatively quickly. A national company ensures name recognition if you later decide to start your own consulting practice. A national company also offers a salary about twice what you would receive if you worked for a smaller local consulting firm. You will probably have twice as much pressure as well.

As a subcontractor. Rather than become an employee, you could subcontract with one or several firms. You would have a less secure position than you would as an employee, but you would also have more flexibility, gain rich experience, and develop a sense of the market.

As a part-timer. If you're not ready to take the plunge, you could consult part-time and keep your existing job. You could use your vacation time and weekends to conduct small projects. Be certain to keep your employer informed of any part-time consulting work. This arrangement is perfect for university professors or individuals who have vacation time or free time on weekends for additional work.

As a partner. You could enter a partnership with one or more other consultants. You would be able to share the burden of expenses, marketing, and workload. The greatest drawback to this arrangement is the potential for conflict over business and personal preferences. These conflicts can vary from an unbalanced workload, to communication, to how much to charge. In the past couple of years, I have advised a number of virtual partnerships: the partners have their own office or locations, and many are located in different states. They come together periodically for synergy or to use specific expertise to collaborate on different projects.

As a self-employed consultant. Starting your own consulting business is what this book is about. This is certainly the greatest risk among the choices, but it also presents the greatest potential payoff.

How do you rate the five options? Perhaps if you have discovered that you do not have quite enough capital to start your own business now, one of the first four options might appeal to you temporarily. If you are not quite ready to leave your job altogether, you could try your hand at part-time consulting. Note here the specific way you will move into consulting:

Discussions with Your Boss

Once you know you would like to move into consulting, make your boss your ally. Except in unusual situations where your boss is not approachable or your organization is not open to employees who want to strike out on their own, it will be helpful to you to meet with your boss to share your future plans. Use these suggestions to have a discussion that will boost your chances for a successful transition to consulting:

- No matter what stage you are in when you have your first discussion, be honest and candid about your plans. This common courtesy will most likely work in your favor.

- If you have developed your business plan, share it with your boss, and ask for input. Often striking out on your own is a dream other people have but have not acted on for various reasons. I have found that they often enjoy living vicariously through those of us who have acted on our dreams. Your boss may be one of those people.

- Keep your boss informed about your progress and to act as a sounding board for your ideas.

- Take care that you are not infringing on your employer's time as you plan for your future. That means you may wish to update your boss over lunch or after work hours as opposed to doing this during the workday. Remember to be a loyal, productive employee to the end.

- Do not bring up the fact that you might be able to consult with your current department or company. Although it is a great transition into consulting, it can appear to be a conflict of interest at this stage of your planning. It may appear to some that you and your boss are planning how to finance your business venture to the disadvantage your current employer.

- Take care that you do not share your plans with too many people beyond your boss. Continue to maintain excellent working relations with your boss and others in your organization. You are probably excited about the prospects for your future as a consultant, but don't let your exuberance take over the office and your main purpose for being at this job.

- Guard against the short-timer attitude as you finish your duties or projects. Being professional straight through to the end gives you the best send-off as a professional consultant.

Determine Your Transition Plan

Making a transition from being a full-time employee to consulting will require some adjustment. A transition plan will help prepare you and those around you for a different lifestyle.

How Will You Transition to Your New Professional Life?

The ideal scenario is that your employer will offer you an opportunity to continue working on a project basis. The current shortage of employees has been a factor in creating that opportunity and is a win-win for you and your employer: you receive a guaranteed income, and your employer receives your knowledge and experience while you both make the transition.

What should you expect if you do this? Many make the transition with 60 percent of their salary or more and work less than 35 percent of the time. The rest of the time can be spent in setting up an office and in marketing.

Another option is working part-time at both your job and at consulting. This is the least appealing of all the options, though, because you will constantly be pulled in different directions. You will be thinking about consulting when you should be working for your employer and concerned about your employer when you should be developing a marketing plan. And it undoubtedly will happen that the first consulting job you land will conflict with your company's annual meeting or some other important event that you must show up for.

A second transition issue is to consider how you feel about being a one-person company. For example, how will you respond the first time a client asks you about the size of your company? How will you feel about saying, "One. Me. That's it." Will you be proud of having gone out on your own? Or is there some stigma about being a consultant—and a lone one at that? How will you feel about doing your own typing, copying, errands, dusting, vacuuming, and trash removal? Another transition consideration is to have a plan ready to implement should you become ill. Could someone fill in for you? Under what circumstances?

A separate but related professional issue you may need to consider is working alone. Right now it probably sounds wonderful: you'll get to make all the decisions, do what you want when you want, and receive all the recognition. The drawback, of course, is that you would also assume all the risk, be responsible for all expenses, and have no one readily available with whom to discuss ideas and issues. A good idea is to set your support network up now. Whom will you call when you want ideas? Whom will you call when you want sound business advice? Whom will you call when you are overwhelmed? And whom will you call when you just want to go to lunch with someone who understands what you are feeling? Make a list now of your support network:

-
-
-
-
-
-
-

What Personal Transitions Will You and Your Family Make?

When everything goes smoothly, your family will readily accept your new role. Having a home office sounds great. Get up when you want, brew a pot of your favorite coffee, write a proposal in a sweatshirt and jeans, no traffic hassle. But how will your family deal with you underfoot all day long? How supportive will your family be when the big deal doesn't come through and you need to dig deeper into the family savings? How supportive will they be when you once again need to pass up a family outing because you must work on Saturday? How will they deal with getting business telephone calls at all hours of the night? You need your family's support—100 percent of it. You do not want them to say, "We told you so!" if something goes wrong.

Here are some transition considerations you all might need to discuss for a smooth change:

- How will you control household noise, such as your dog barking, during "business hours"?

- How will you have privacy when you are working?

- How will everyone share the house to meet everyone's needs? For example, what happens when eight five-year-olds are expected for a birthday party and you are in the middle of a long and important call?

- How will the family feel when you are late for dinner because your project is taking longer than you anticipated, yet you're only in the spare bedroom?

- How will Grandma feel sleeping on the couch because you have taken over the guest room as your office?

- How will your spouse react upon seeing the mess you made in the kitchen for a fast lunch—and didn't clean up?

- How will you deal with the ever-growing lawn outside your window when you have two proposals that are due this week?

- Will you be able to avoid the refrigerator as you walk past it for the twentieth time in one day?

In the space below, make a list of agreements you and your family will consider as part of your transition.

Where Will the Money Come From?

Even if you leave your job with the promise of six months of work, there is no guarantee that you will have your next projects lined up when that income stream ends.

You may become so tied up in the project your former employer has extended to you that you may not find the time to conduct the marketing that you should. Or your family may decide that you must take a vacation before you launch your new business. Or you may have been on the marketing warpath and have lots of possibilities, but nothing has materialized yet.

If you plunge right in to your new business without the benefit of support from your former employer, you will most likely need cash to start your business. Few people set aside enough money to start a business, no matter how far in advance they plan.

Where will the money come from? Consider these options:

- You could take money from your savings account.

- You could borrow against your retirement account (you can do this only if you'll continue working with your employer).

- You could obtain a loan on the equity in your house.

- You could borrow against your life insurance policy.

- If you have stocks, you could go on margin against them.

- You could obtain a line of credit from your bank.

- Your spouse could increase his or her contribution.

- You could sell something of value, such as a motor home or sailboat.

- You could cut back on some of your spending—for example, by not taking a vacation.

- You could obtain a business bank loan.

- You could apply for a loan from the Small Business Administration.

- You could ask a friend or colleague to sponsor you.

- You could borrow against your credit card (don't do this unless you have a great opportunity in hand and can pay it off quickly).

List all of your options and the amount that is available from each here:

Options Available   *How Much Money*

Based on your personal cash flow projections in Chapter Two and your business plan in Chapter Five, what shortfall do you expect over the next twelve months? What source will fund the shortage?

Month   *Shortage*   *Source of Funds*

Will you have enough money to easily get through the year? Have you planned for a worst-case scenario? You should be optimistic because positive thinking can take you a long way, but remember that it can't pay the grocery bill. You will be successful, but it may take longer than you anticipated.

Personal Financial Statement

If you think you may require a loan or expect to apply for a line of credit, you will need to provide a financial statement that summarizes your net worth. Most banks expect you to update it annually. A sample Personal Financial Statement is provided.

Examine the issues identified in this chapter. Are you ready to make the move? What do you need to put in place?

Personal Financial Statement

Assets

Cash	_____
Savings accounts	_____
Stocks, bonds, and other securities	_____
Accounts, notes	_____
Life insurance (cash value)	_____
Rebates, refunds	_____
Autos, other vehicles	_____
Real estate	_____
Vested pension plan or retirement accounts	_____
Other assets	_____

Total Assets _____

Liabilities

Accounts payable	_____
Real estate loans	_____
Other liabilities	_____

Total Liabilities _____

Total Assets Less Total Liabilities = Net Worth _____

Source: The Consultant's Quick Start Guide: An Action Plan for Your First Year in Business, Second Edition. Copyright 2009 by John Wiley & Sons, Inc. Reproduced by permission of Pfeiffer, an Imprint of Wiley. www.pfeiffer.com (originally from Biech, 2007).

ACTION

Plan with Your Family

Sit down with your spouse, significant other, or other family members and discuss the issues identified in this chapter. How supportive will everyone be of your endeavor? Ask everyone in the discussion to identify what excites them the most about your planned consulting role. Also ask them what concerns them the most. Capture these responses here. Then as a family, decide how you can build on the positives and what you can do to address the concerns.

What excites you the most about my becoming a consultant?

What concerns you about my becoming a consultant?

How can we build on the positives?

What can we do to address your concerns?

· ·

This chapter, although not dealing directly with developing your business, is one of the most important ones in this book. A successful transition plan is like a well-orchestrated football play. Planning ahead and thinking through all the possibilities are critical to a successful transition. Involve your family and others in the planning up-front.

Quick Start LISTS

Actions I Will Take

Ideas I Have

Questions I Have

Setting Up Your Office

In this chapter you will

- Explore your options for an office location
- Prepare a plan to set up your office
- Learn how to manage your paperwork, including record keeping and invoicing

Office Location Options

You have many options when it comes to setting up your office. You could rent a standard office, lease space in an executive suite, or set up a home office. No matter where your office is, ensure that it projects the professional image you wish.

Renting Office Space

An office in a nice office building at a recognized location adds to your appearance as a professional. You may also feel more professional leaving your house every morning for the workplace. Leasing office space is often a long-term commitment (as long as three to five years), and if office space is in high demand, it could be costly as well.

Sharing Executive Suites

An option that lies somewhere between a full-blown office and your spare bedroom is an office in an executive suite. The popularity of these suites has grown due to the cost savings that are available by sharing a conference room, office support, telephone systems, and copy machines. Executive suites run the gamut for amenities, service, and quality, so shop around. Ask existing tenants about their satisfaction with services they receive.

Using a Home Office

Just a short time ago, working out of your home was not cool. You would have been viewed as less than professional and not serious about your career. Today, all that has changed. Flexi-place, flex-time, and telecommuting arrangements are on the rise, and those who work at home are often envied by those who cannot.

Examine the advantages of having your office in your home:

- You work where you live.
- You have the flexibility of using time as you choose for both your business and your personal life, getting up at midnight to add an idea to your proposal or being available to receive delivery of the new family television.
- You can deduct from your taxes a proportionate amount of your home's utility costs, taxes, mortgage, or rent.
- It's a low-cost option for start-ups that minimizes your risk.
- You don't have to commute.

There are also some disadvantages to having your office in your home:

- You work where you live.
- It may be inconvenient for meeting clients.
- There are many distractions, including chores, the refrigerator, television, and your hobbies.
- You may be lonely if you are accustomed to working in a large office with many people around.

- You may need to overcome the stigma of working out of your home if clients expect you to work out of an office.

- Creating dedicated space may be difficult.

Notice that "you work where you live" is both an advantage and a disadvantage. The choice really boils down to whether it is the right decision for you.

No Office at All

Most consultants provide their services at the client's place of business, so you do have the broadest of choices for office location. In fact, I spoke with one savvy young man recently who was certain that he did not need an office at all for the kind of consulting he did. He held up his laptop and his cell phone and said, "With these I can do everything I need to for my clients at any location!"

Indeed, no office at all is certainly an option in today's world.

Weighing Your Options

You have other options in addition to the four listed. You could share office space with someone or sublease from others. In both of these cases, you will want to maintain your own separate identity for legal and professional reasons.

Answer these questions to help you decide the best option for you.

How much space do you need?

How much can you afford to pay for office space?

Is location important to your business?

What image must you project? To whom?

How long can you commit to stay?

How often will you be in your office?

Set Up Your Office

Once you've decided on space, you will need to ensure that you have furnished, equipped, wired, and supplied it with everything you will need.

An Office Is an Office, Not Your Family Room

This may seem like a strong statement, but if you have chosen the home office route, heed the warning. It may be cute when your four-year-old answers the telephone; it's not cute when the caller is the CEO you met at last week's conference. And the first time your dog barks as you are talking to a prospective client, you may understand why you must separate your office from the rest of the house. Install separate telephone lines for your office as one of the first things you do. You may want two: one for faxing and a second for voice calls. You can probably share your Internet service provider, but check into this to be sure.

Furnishing Your Office

Once you've settled on office space, you will need to furnish it with at least a desk, chairs, bookshelves, and a four-drawer filing cabinet. While you're planning, think about where you will place the fax machine, telephone, answering machine, computer and printer, and copy machine. Will you need extra tables on which to place some of these items?

Use the grid on the next page to lay out your office space. Each square counts as one foot. Mark where the windows are located. Then measure your larger pieces of furniture and start sketching—with a pencil. While you're doing this, also plan where you will need outlets and extra telephone jacks. And very important—lighting. Where's the natural lighting? Will you need additional lamps?

Planning Your Technical Needs

You will most likely need a computer and printer, fax machine, telephone system, and answering machine. What about a copy machine? A lease can be reasonable, but if there is a copy shop or a printer near you, you may not be concerned about it immediately. You will also wish to invest in a business cell phone. You may use your personal cell phone for business and simply change the way that you answer it. And how

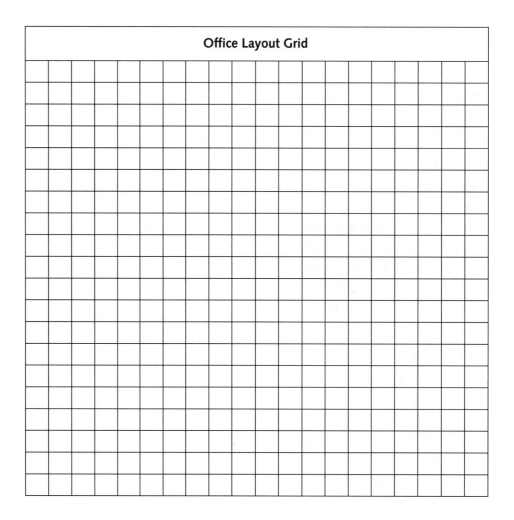

Office Layout Grid

about a PDA or pager? You will need to decide what you will need. My advice is to try to condense as much as possible to as few pieces of equipment as possible.

Get Wired. Accommodate all those electronic items with plenty of grounded outlets (if your home is not new, you may need to have some wiring completed) and telephone jacks (at least two separate lines: one for your fax machine and the other for a telephone). Don't forget a coaxial television cable if you are hooked up to a cable modem for Internet access.

About Your Answering Machine. The outgoing message on your answering machine should sound professional and as much like voice mail as possible: no distracting noise in the background (like your latest CD), no long series of beeps before the caller can leave a message, no unprofessional melodic chimes. The caller should be able to leave a message of any length. Your outgoing message is part of your image; it sells you.

Change your message daily to let people know where you are. A generic message of, "I'm sorry I missed your call. Please leave a message and I'll get back to you as soon as I can," tells the caller nothing. Are you on another line? Are you off to the post office for ten minutes? Are you on a two-week cruise? The best messages are up-to-date: "Hello, this is Carlos. Today is Tuesday, May 13, and I will be in meetings most of the day. I will pick up my messages at the end of the day and return your call no later than Wednesday morning. Thank you for calling!"

One dilemma for many consultants is that we are with clients during the day and unable to answer telephone calls, even if others call on our cell phones. This is why I generally provide my office number to clients. They can call and reach a live person who can either tell them what I am doing and how soon they can expect a response, and in an emergency, my office staff can always reach me. If you will not have an office with support staff, you may at some point wish to switch to an answering service.

Supplying Your Office

When it comes time to purchase the office supplies you will need, there are two possible approaches. You can start with the following office shopping list and add other things to it. Or you can go to your local office supply store, grab a shopping cart, and walk up and down the aisles until you've found everything you think you will need. No matter which method you use, you will probably forget something. One last thing: Where are you going to store all these supplies?

Office Shopping List

☐ Paper
   ☐ lined
   ☐ note pads
   ☐ computer/printer
   ☐ three-hole punched
   ☐ colors
   ☐ other:

☐ Sticky note pads—size?
☐ Paper clips
☐ Binder clips
☐ Pens

- ☐ Markers
  - ☐ flip chart
  - ☐ small
  - ☐ other:
- ☐ Tape
  - ☐ strapping
  - ☐ cellophane
  - ☐ masking
- ☐ Stapler and staples
- ☐ Three-hole punch
- ☐ Wastebaskets
- ☐ Extension cords
- ☐ Tape dispenser
- ☐ Surge protectors
- ☐ Calculator
- ☐ Stacking bins
- ☐ Bookends
- ☐ Banker boxes
- ☐ Pencil holder
- ☐ Flip chart pads
- ☐ File folders
- ☐ Pocket folders
- ☐ Envelopes
- ☐ Desk lamps
- ☐ Index cards
- ☐ Clock
- ☐ Dictionary
- ☐ Thesaurus
- ☐ Calendar
- ☐ Coffee cup
- ☐ Pencils
- ☐ Erasers
- ☐ Rubber cement
- ☐ Rubber bands
- ☐ Labels
- ☐ Stamp dispenser
- ☐ Scissors
- ☐ Letter opener
- ☐ Scale to weigh mail
- ☐ Other things:

Stop at your post office to pick up these additional supplies:

- ☐ Stamps
- ☐ Priority mail folders
- ☐ Priority mail boxes
- ☐ Priority mail envelopes
- ☐ Express mail supplies

Paper, Paper Everywhere!

Consulting is not a paperless profession! You will use, throw away, send, sell, deliver, stamp, write on, print, read, and file more paper than you can imagine. Start a system early to keep yourself organized.

Establishing a Filing System

Develop a filing system that works for you. File things with two important aspects in mind: ease of putting them away and ease of finding them! We use different colors of files to distinguish what's inside: blue for project files, yellow for office files, red for client resource and information, green for volunteer activities, tan for resources such as articles. You may start out with just one drawer and file everything alphabetically. Once you have been in business for several months, you will probably want to separate your drawers into categories, such as past client folders, originals, proposals, and resources.

Good Filing Habits

- Grab a file as soon as you start a new project, client, or another category.
- Write the same thing first on each file tab; usually that means the organization or key word. If the file is about Mr. Hendrix from the San Francisco branch of Wells Fargo Bank, the file could be under H, S, or W. Decide what it's going to be now, and be sure to stick with it.
- Put everything back in its place after you are finished with it, or . . .
- Store your filing in a small basket. Once the basket is filled or Friday rolls around—whichever comes first—file everything.
- Avoid duplicate files.
- Do not file meaningless attachments.
- Condense your materials; that is, after a project, toss anything that will not be useful later.
- Purge your files regularly—at least once each year.

Establishing Your Record-Keeping System

Your records are the voice of your success. Good records can do two things for you:

- They will tell you whether you are financially successful.
- They will help keep you organized.

Quick TIP

You might want to organize your desk drawer with monthly dividers. This method can help you keep organized and see at a glance what you have coming up in the months ahead.

After six months in business, your records should be speaking to you. They will tell you:

- Your total income and expenses
- Your profit or loss
- The number of customers you served
- The profit margins for each customer
- The accuracy of your projections
- How much money you will need for the next six months
- What you need to do to increase your business

Many of the forms you need were discussed in Chapters Three and Five. The forms that follow in this chapter will round out what you need to tell you how you're doing financially and to keep you organized.

Electronic Records

Select your financial record-keeping system early. This chapter provides you with some basic forms; most accounting software will be able to generate the same information easily for you. You might consider using Peach Tree, QuickBooks Pro, One-Write Plus, or MYOB (Mind Your Own Business).

Consult your accountant when you select accounting software, so that your software will be compatible. Your accountant will also be able to assist you with setting it up so that it is useful to both of you and can be shared electronically.

Monthly Expense Worksheet/Record. This record is one that I examine regularly. I create a budget at the beginning of each year based on the past year and the projections for the upcoming year. You have already created a budget in Chapter Three. This form tells you whether you are taking in more or less income each month than you projected and whether your expenses are at the same level you projected. The implications are clear. See the sample form.

Monthly Expense Worksheet/Record

Account	Budget	Jan	Feb	Mar	April	May	June	July	Aug	Sept	Oct	Nov	Dec	Total
Accounting, banking, legal fees														
Advertising and marketing														
Automobile expenses														
Books and resources														
Clerical support														
Copying and printing														
Donations														
Dues and subscriptions														
Entertainment														
Equipment leases														
Insurance														
Interest and loans														
Licenses														
Meals														
Office supplies														
Postage														
Professional development														
Professional fees														
Rent														
Repairs and maintenance														
Retirement plan														
Salaries														
Seminar expenses														
Taxes														
Telephone														
Travel														
Utilities														
Total														

Source: The Consultant's Quick Start Guide: An Action Plan for Your First Year in Business, Second Edition. Copyright 2009 by John Wiley & Sons, Inc. Reproduced by permission of Pfeiffer, an Imprint of Wiley. www.pfeiffer.com (originally from Biech, 2007).

Petty Cash Record. This is a simple way to track your petty cash at the end of each month. It will save you time when you try coming up with all those receipts for your accountant. See the sample Petty Cash Record.

Petty Cash Record					
				From: _____	To: _____

Date	Where Bought	Item(s) Purchased	Expense Category	Initial	Amount
				Total	

Source: The Consultant's Quick Start Guide: An Action Plan for Your First Year in Business, Second Edition. Copyright 2009 by John Wiley & Sons, Inc. Reproduced by permission of Pfeiffer, an Imprint of Wiley. www.pfeiffer.com (originally from Biech, 2007).

Revenue Projections. This form will track the dollar amount of the work you will do each month. It is critical for projecting cash flow. Use a form similar to the one provided here.

Revenue Projections

Organization and Project	Jan	Feb	Mar	April	May	June	July	Aug	Sept	Oct	Nov	Dec	Total
Total Revenue													

Source: The Consultant's Quick Start Guide: An Action Plan for Your First Year in Business, Second Edition. Copyright 2009 by John Wiley & Sons, Inc. Reproduced by permission of Pfeiffer, an Imprint of Wiley. www.pfeiffer.com (originally from Biech, 2007).

Invoicing. If you want clients to pay you, you need to bill them. The next two forms provided here establish your invoicing process. The first is a sample of what is on an invoice (the bill you send to your client). The second (Invoice Summary) is a form to track whether clients paid you and when.

Invoice

INVOICE
100-000111-20XX

TO: Mr. Dale Woodward
  Gilbert Manufacturing
  333 Ridge Road
  Anywhere, NY 10000

Invoice Date: January 24, 20XX

For: Presented "Talent Management Applied: Learning from Our Experience" for Gilbert Manufacturing
  November 15, 20XX
  Elizabeth Drake, Facilitator
    Facilitator Fee $4,000.00

EXPENSES: Mileage Round Trip to Airport:
    80 miles @ $.50 per mile .... $ 40.00
  Airfare .... $ 710.00
  Airport parking .... $ 30.00
  Lodging... $ 190.00
  Books .... $ 0.00
    Expense Total .... $ 970.00

Amount Due: $4,970.00

Terms: Due upon receipt

Payable to: ebb associates
  Box 8249
  Norfolk, VA 12503

  Federal ID# 33-5333788

  2 percent late fee charged per month for accounts due over 15 days

Source: The Consultant's Quick Start Guide: An Action Plan for Your First Year in Business, Second Edition. Copyright 2009 by John Wiley & Sons, Inc. Reproduced by permission of Pfeiffer, an Imprint of Wiley. www.pfeiffer.com (originally from Biech, 2007).

Invoice Summary

Work Date	Organization	Trainer	Invoice Number	Date Billed	Date Paid	Facilitator Fee	Materials Fee	Expenses	Total Fee
Total									

Source: The Consultant's Quick Start Guide: An Action Plan for Your First Year in Business, Second Edition. Copyright 2009 by John Wiley & Sons, Inc. Reproduced by permission of Pfeiffer, an Imprint of Wiley. www.pfeiffer.com (originally from Biech, 2007).

Measuring Profitability. The Project Profitability form will help you measure your profitability. It tracks how much time you spent on the development or design, or both, and delivery of each project.

Project Profitability				
Project Title	**Company Name**	**Development Time**	**Development Cost**	**Income**

Source: The Consultant's Quick Start Guide: An Action Plan for Your First Year in Business, Second Edition. Copyright 2009 by John Wiley & Sons, Inc. Reproduced by permission of Pfeiffer, an Imprint of Wiley. www.pfeiffer.com

Staying Organized

The next two forms will help you stay organized.

Session Planner. This form will help you organize before going off to a client's location to work on a project.

Session Planner

Date: _____ Company: _____
Topic: _____
Contact Person: _____ Phone Number: _____
Purchase Order: _____ Fee: _____
Speaker/Presenter/Consultant: _____
Time Held: _____ Number of Participants: _____
Where Held: Address: _____
             Building: _____
             Room: _____
             Directions: _____

Travel: Hotel: _____
          Daytime Phone: _____ Nighttime Phone: _____
          Directions:

Equipment: _____ Computer   _____ DVD player
            _____ LED Projector and Screen   _____ Flip Chart(s) and Markers
            _____ Other: _____

Room Configuration: _____

Confirmation with Company: [ ] By Phone   [ ] By E-mail
[ ] Date   [ ] Number of Participants [ ] Address/Location
[ ] Hotel Arrangements   [ ] Equipment Needs   [ ] Room Configuration
[ ] Consultant Arrival Time [ ] Purchase Order Number

Materials: Binders: [ ] Type: _____
          Folders: [ ] Type: _____
                  [ ] Personalized Seals   [ ] Business Cards
          Unbound: [ ] 3-Hole Punch   [ ] Staple   [ ] Other: _____

Supplies: _____ Table Tents _____ Name Tags _____ Markers _____ Trainer's Manual
        [ ] Other: _____

Special Instructions: _____

Source: The Consultant's Quick Start Guide: An Action Plan for Your First Year in Business, Second Edition. Copyright 2009 by John Wiley & Sons, Inc. Reproduced by permission of Pfeiffer, an Imprint of Wiley. www.pfeiffer.com (originally from Biech, 2007).

Library Sign-Out Sheet. Use this form if you love to loan out your books, but you like it even more when they are returned.

Library Sign-Out Sheet				
Book	Borrowed By	Date	Will Return By	Returned

Source: The Consultant's Quick Start Guide: An Action Plan for Your First Year in Business, Second Edition. Copyright 2009 by John Wiley & Sons, Inc. Reproduced by permission of Pfeiffer, an Imprint of Wiley. www.pfeiffer.com (originally from Biech, 2007).

Preparing Forms

Make twelve copies of each of the forms you will need; then store them in one of the yellow folders you just bought during your office shopping trip. If you have the second edition of *The Business of Consulting,* all the forms are on the disk. Just pull it up, personalize it for your business, and print twelve of each. You will note that several forms in this book have been updated since *The Business of Consulting* was published, but they still provide a basis from which to begin.

You've identified an office location, prepared a plan to set up your office, and established your record-keeping system. Now all you need are clients. Chapter Eight will guide you through that challenge.

Quick Start LISTS

Actions I Will Take

Ideas I Have

Questions I Have

Finding Clients

In this chapter you will

- Determine your niche in the market
- Analyze your competition
- Identify your first clients
- Create a plan to land your first work

Determine Your Market Niche

In Chapter One you declared that you were a _____ consultant who helps your clients to _____, which benefits them _____. We'll begin with this statement as you identify your market niche.

Your *niche* is the position you wish to occupy that sets you apart from as many other consultants as possible. This niche may be based on the type of service or product you provide, the type of client or industry you serve, how you provide your services, or the specific expertise or experience you have that validates your services.

So far you have explored your areas of expertise, the experience you've had, your natural abilities, the benefits you could provide a client, the results that might be valuable to a client, and other things. To identify your niche in the marketplace, you will examine what you will do from a client's perspective and begin to describe your clients more specifically, thus homing in on your potential client base.

To what part of the market will you offer your consulting? You need to clarify this before you create your marketing plan in the next chapter. A portion of your marketing plan will target a market segment on which you will focus your marketing efforts. You need this focus so that you are not trying to be everything to everyone.

The opportunities available to you as a consultant are broad. You must begin to identify your niche—what you profess to do. This is a long-time consulting dilemma: if what you claim you can do is too broad, your expertise may appear shallow; if what you state you do is too narrow, it decreases your chances for locating work. To say it another way, the more generalized you are, the less credible you'll be in potential clients' eyes; the more specialized you are, the more difficult it is to obtain business.

Even understanding this, you must still determine what sets you apart from other consultants. What is unique about what you offer? A new consulting company can be successful more easily if it can focus on a specifically defined market. If you are a small company, you will be more successful creating your own niche than trying to compete against larger, more established companies that may be your competitors.

When ebb associates started in the late 1970s, we decided to offer customized training programs to clients. At the time we didn't really understand that we were selecting a unique niche. What we did know is that most participants in the training sessions we offered complained about not being able to transfer what they learned in a training session to their workplaces. We were able to do what the large training vendors could not: we could focus on one client at a time and design exactly what that client required. Now that desktop publishing is widespread, that service is not so unique. However, at the time, we made our mark in the training consulting field by filling a unique need and along the way identified our niche in the marketplace.

How can you discover and describe your niche? First, review the previous chapters where you focused on what you could offer. Second, determine if potential clients have a need that is not being fulfilled or a gap that is not closed completely by your competitors. Third, identify the services and products that you could deliver to meet the need or close the gap.

This chapter leads you through several exercises to help you uncover your niche. The exercises will help you to explore your expertise and potential client base, present a process to discover what clients need, and suggest how you can scrutinize and compare your competitors.

Begin by using the newspaper industry's method of uncovering the facts—answering the who, what, where, when, and why questions. Answer the questions under each heading that follows to identify your marketing niche and describe your client. Where appropriate, answer these questions from your potential clients' perspective.

Who?

Use these questions to begin to develop a profile of your potential client:

- Will you target for-profit or nonprofit organizations?
- If you target for-profit, what sector will be your focus—for example, manufacturing, service, retail?
- What specific industry will you target—for example, health care, hospitality, food service, construction, high tech?
- If you target nonprofit, what sector will be your focus—for example, associations, educational institutions, or local, state, or federal government?
- What size organizations will you target—for example, Fortune 500, medium, small? You may choose to identify the size by number of employees, revenues, or something that is unique to the industry; hospitals, for example, measure size by the number of beds.
- What level in the organization will you target—for example, frontline employees, first-level supervisors, managers, or executives?
- What's the structure of the group you will target—for example, new teams, intact work groups, individuals?

What?

Use these questions to pull together the expertise and experience that you explored in Chapter One. Now is the time to identify the specifics:

- What will your customers want from you? How will this differ from what they expect from other consultants?

- Will your clients have a special situation—for example, start-up, family-owned, merged, or high-growth businesses?

- What role will your customers see you conducting—for example, trainer, facilitator, coach, technical adviser, process consultant, content expert, support, resource?

- What topic of expertise will your client expect—example, team building, computer programming, leadership, time management, investing, regulatory laws, marine biology, accounting, construction, inventory control?

- What's special that sets you apart from other consultants?

Where?

Part of your work in Chapter Two was to identify where you would ideally like to work. It is probable that clients in your chosen industry may be found everywhere. Therefore, location may have as much to do with your preference as anything else:

- Based on the lifestyle you have described in Chapter Two, where will you be working?

- Will your focus be local, statewide, regional, national, or international?

- Do your selected industries suggest a specific locale, such as furniture manufacturing in North Carolina, high tech in Silicon Valley, importers in San Francisco, New York, and other coastal cities?

- In what surroundings will you work: for example, rural, village, city? What size city (if a city is your choice)?

- Will you narrow your market niche by climate?

When?

These questions will help clarify the time-bound aspects in your consulting niche:

- Will you focus on long-term or shorter contracts?

- What's the range in length of the contracts you will target?

- Will the time range be different for different services?

- Will you provide follow-up services?

- How much repeat business will you target?

- At what point in the problem-solving cycle would you enter—for example, identifying a problem, identifying the cause of the problem, identifying the solution, or implementing the solution?

Why?

In Chapter Three (page 51) you identified the value you add for which a client would be willing to pay. Use that information to help you focus your marketing niche based on why a client would hire you:

- Why would a client view your experience and expertise worthy of hire?

- Why would a client hire you over your competition?

- Why might a client see you as adding flexibility to the organization?

- Why would a client look to you to offer a fresh, objective point of view?

- How efficient do you believe you are?

- Would clients hire you if they needed to reassure regulatory, safety, or legal authorities about something?

Is There a Need?

Without getting into actual market research, it is important to identify whether there is a need for the niche you have just identified. You may have identified a service that enables you to use what you like and what you know, but will the client base you identified want to buy what you offer?

Is There a Client Base?

Before you move forward, be sure that there is a client base ready and waiting for your consulting service or product. Select three organizations that match the characteristics of the organizations you just described. Then follow these steps and record what you learn here.

1. Identify specific individuals in organizations to whom you will eventually sell your services. You can do this by checking the company's annual report (which you can usually obtain on request or by checking the company's Web site) or calling the receptionist and asking for the name of the person in the position to whom you wish to speak.

2. Call the individuals, and tell them that you have a business concept you would like to discuss and about which you would value their opinions. Ask if they have five minutes for you. If not, ask if there is a better time. If the person responds positively, move forward. If the person responds negatively, say thanks, and move to your next candidate.

3. Briefly explain your business, its purpose, and how it might benefit the individuals and their businesses.

4. Ask whether they think they would see a need for your services in the future. Probe to find out why they responded the way that they did.

5. Thank them for their time.

6. If they responded positively, ask them if you could send more information, a letter, or a brochure once your company is up and running. (This might be your first marketing action—and perhaps your first client. My first exploratory visit turned into my first paying client.)

7. Be sure to follow up with a handwritten thank you note on the same day you made the phone call.

8. Record your information:

Company Name/Individual	Position	Response
1.		
2.		
3.		

Analyze Your Call

Did the phone calls encourage or discourage you? If you are positive about moving forward, spend some time analyzing your competition next. If the phone calls were not positive, you might analyze your calls. Did you call the right people? Did you call the right companies? Should you call others? Did you sell your concept well? Was the timing right? Did everything go as you planned it? What might you do differently with subsequent calls?

● ●

Who's Your Competition?

Know Your Industry

Keep an eye on your competition. Being a consultant can be lonely, and this means you may find yourself outside the information loop—what's happening in the industry in which you work and in business in general. You may find being alone psychologically difficult; it can also be financially devastating if you do not stay on top of what's happening in your field. What's happening in the field and what your competition does will affect your marketing direction.

Be aware of trends. How will a surge in downsizing affect your consulting services? How will the latest management fad affect the message you deliver to your clients? How will changes in technology affect your products and service?

How are your clients addressing these changes? You can observe this with what you already have available. Read your professional journals with these questions in mind: Who's advertising? What are they selling? What's their focus? Who's writing articles? What are the topics? Attend conferences with these questions in mind: Who's presenting? What are they expounding? What's the buzz in the hallways? Attend trade shows: Who has a booth? What are they selling? What message are they delivering? Visit bookstores: Who's writing? What topics are being published?

Take time now and page through your most recent professional journal. What did you learn about your competition from reading it?

Know Your Competition

Review the information from your business plan in Chapter Five to get you started here. You need to understand your competition so that you can set yourself apart from it. You will want a clear sense of what differentiates you from your competition before you write your marketing plan in Chapter Nine.

Identify three competitors, and complete the Competitor Comparison chart so you can compare your business to the competition.

Competitor Comparison

	Your Practice	Competitor 1	Competitor 2	Competitor 3
Name				
Location				
Fees Charged				
Time in Business				
Specialty Area				
Client Type				
Client Location				
Why Clients Use Them				
Name Recognition				
Image				
Quality				
Other				

Source: The Consultant's Quick Start Guide: An Action Plan for Your First Year in Business, Second Edition. Copyright 2009 by John Wiley & Sons, Inc. Reproduced by permission of Pfeiffer, an Imprint of Wiley. www.pfeiffer.com

Quick  **TIP**

Use Your Network

If you are unable to answer the questions above about your industry, tap into your network. You might talk to friends in business, your potential clients, or another consultant who is outside your geographical or content area. Professional organizations also provide opportunities to talk with your competitors at conferences and chapter meetings. You should belong to at least two professional organizations that support what you do.

Competitive Analysis

Use the data you uncovered to organize your thoughts about your competition:

Who are your strongest competitors?

In which geographical areas will you have the most competition? The least? What does this tell you about where to focus your energy to get new clients?

How do your competitors' specialty areas compare with yours? How will this affect your ability to generate business?

How will your competitors' pricing affect your ability to get business?

How will your competitors' experience, name recognition, image, and reputation for quality affect your ability to compete? How might you take advantage of this in finding new clients?

What are your competitors doing right? What could you do better?

What might you be able to offer that differentiates you from your competitors?

Your Niche

Examine everything you have identified about you, the clients you will target, and your competitors. How would you summarize the niche you have selected for yourself? What is special about your services that sets you apart from the rest? How are you defining your client base that sets you apart?

Use these questions as a guide to write your niche statement here.

Identify Your First Clients

You have clarified your niche. Now it's time to specify the organizations in that niche by name. Who will be your first clients?

You are in control of identifying your first clients. Yes, you will acquire some work through referrals from friends, family, and colleagues. You may have some work from your current (or past) employer. And you may have some work come your way through people you meet at professional meetings or conferences. Some of this work may be related to your niche, but much of it may not. As you begin, however, you will most likely not turn any of it down.

Examine the niche statement you wrote at the end of the previous section. Now identify twenty organizations by name that meet your criteria and with which you would like to do business. This is not the time to be shy, timid, or modest. Go for it. Are you thinking that Microsoft is too large? Perhaps Harvard is too prestigious? Or General Motors is too impenetrable? Don't let size, prestige, or reputation scare you. The people who manage organizations need good consulting, no matter what the size of the company supplying it. I've always said, "Go for the big fish; you'll spend the same time baiting the hook." You will invest the same amount of time marketing to large organizations as small, and the payoff may be much greater.

Larger organizations have larger consulting budgets, they generally have a greater need, they are more likely to hire for repeat work, and they are often willing to take a risk with new consultants. So don't be intimidated by size. To whom do you want to provide your consulting services? Identify twenty organizations here that you would like to hire you as a consultant:

1.

2.

3.

4.

5.

6.

7.

8.

9.

10.

11.

12.

13.

14.

15.

16.

17.

18.

19.

20.

Land Your First Work

You've identified your twenty top candidates. Now how do you get to them? You could just make a phone call and talk to them. That's called *cold calling,* and usually isn't much fun. I have a friend in sales who lives by cold calls. He says he makes one hundred phone calls to find ten people who will talk to him. Of those ten, two will agree to meet with him in person, and one will purchase his product. That doesn't sound like fun to me.

There is a way to warm up those cold calls. And although the process takes some investment up front, the odds of an immediate sale are much greater, you will begin to build relationships for future sales, and it's much more fun.

Here's the process I use:

1. Identify twenty or thirty organizations you wish to target. Begin with that many because some will fall out along the way: you may have difficulty locating information about them, or you may change your mind about wanting to work with them based on information you learn.

2. Copy one Company Profile form for each organization you have targeted. Complete whatever information you know about it.

Company Profile

Company Name _____

Address _____

_____

Telephone _____   Web site _____

Employees _____

Management Positions

_____   _____

_____   _____

_____   _____

_____   _____

Products and Services _____

_____

History _____

_____

_____

Financial Information _____

_____

Organizational Philosophy _____

_____

Relationship to My Consulting Services _____

_____

Additional Relevant Information _____

_____

Resources Used _____

3. Next check out the organization's Web site. Capture all the information that might be pertinent to services you could offer the organization. You are trying to gather enough information for two reasons: first, to learn as much as you can about the organization, and second, to have enough information to compose a unique, personalized letter that will grab the reader's attention.

4. If the organization is publicly traded, you should be able to obtain the annual report.

5. Use the Company Profile form to organize the information you find.

6. You probably will not get all that you need from the Web site. Therefore, you will continue your research at other sites. First, conduct a general search on the Internet. This may uncover a wide variety of information—some useful, some not. Continue searching for what you need.

7. If you still need more information, you may be able to find information at your library. If you are researching a local company, check the local business magazines, journals and periodicals, local business newsletters, local newspaper, the city directory, manufacturer and business directories, and any other useful resources. Each of these has an index that makes it easy to research a list of clients in a couple of hours. If you can't find it on the Internet, your friendly local librarian is sure to assist.

8. Once you have gathered all your information, compose a letter to each of these clients. Follow these guidelines:

   • Be certain you are sending the letter to the right person.

   • Double-check the person's title and spelling of the name.

   • Focus on the recipient in the first paragraph, and show you know what's important to the organization.

   • In the next one or two paragraphs, connect the recipient to the need for consulting services and establish your qualifications. You must customize these paragraphs as well. For example, a list of your experiences should relate to the recipient's need or industry. If you can't do that yet due to a lack of experience, provide your most impressive information to date, but relate it to the potential client.

- In the final paragraph, tell the person what to expect. Maintain control of the process by saying, "I will call you within the week to schedule an appointment to . . ."

9. Mail your letter, and follow up as promised.

I've used this process for over twenty years with remarkable success. I usually find enough information for about half the potential clients I target. Ninety-five percent of all recipients are interested enough to speak to me, and more than half of them agree to meet me within the month. Of those, half become clients within a year. The rest become contacts, resources, or clients in the future because I stay in touch with them.

You can have this same success rate. And you will find that this is a very positive way to begin a client-consultant relationship.

The Sample Letter is a sample of the type that I use to contact potential clients. Other letters using this same format can be found in the second edition of *The Business of Consulting* (2007).

Sample Letter

July 12, 20XX

Robert R. Birkhauser, President
Auto Glass Specialists, Inc.
2810 Syene Road
Madison, WI 53713

Dear Mr. Birkhauser:

Auto Glass Specialists is one of Madison's phenomenons. In just over twenty years you have transformed an innovative idea into a successful business spanning five states. Your expertise for repairing windows in cars, trucks, and heavy equipment is now available in twenty-three locations, with sales pushing $40 million. Strong management and hard-working employees achieved these results.

At ebb associates we recognize the important role the employee plays in the successful growth of any company. Further, we have found that improving employees' communication skills results in improved productivity and increased profit. Do you realize that just one five-hundred-dollar listening mistake by each of Auto Glass Specialists' four-hundred employees can result in a loss of $200,000 each year? Improved communication skills can decrease mistakes, increase your profits, and improve customer relations.

ebb associates specializes in communication training. We present workshops and seminars focusing on improved communication and will custom-design a program to meet your needs at Auto Glass Specialists. Our clients, including Tenneco Automotive and Cardinal Glass, recognize our commitment to meeting their needs, providing excellent follow-up, and obtaining results. We'd like to help you, too, so that you can improve the quality and increase the quantity of work by maximizing the potential of your human resources.

I would like to call you within the week to schedule an appointment to discuss how we can assist you to meet your goals at Auto Glass Specialists. I am enclosing a list of the course titles that we can customize to meet your specific needs. I look forward to meeting and working with you.

Sincerely,

Elaine Biech
ebb associates

Source: Biech, *The Business of Consulting,* 2nd ed., 2007.

What About the Referrals You've Received?

Do follow up with every referral you receive from friends, family, and colleagues. Even if the project is not quite right for you now, the meeting may lead to other work in the future. And you may also ask potential clients to refer you to someone who might be able to use your services. (This is networking at its finest.)

Select one referral right now, and make an appointment to explore possibilities. You will find this meeting helpful in several ways. First, you will get an idea of what to expect when you visit a potential client. Second, you will have an opportunity to practice selling your services. Third, you will learn what needs clarification as you describe what you do.

You Have an Appointment—Now What?

Okay, you have an appointment with a client. What do you need to know before you go? Be sure you know at least the following: the meeting purpose, who will attend, how long the meeting will last, and exactly where it will be (office, conference room, and so forth). What do you do once you get in the door?

Your initial meeting is critical. It sets a tone for the rest of your relationship. You may come prepared with a PowerPoint presentation, materials in a bound folder, and a precisely worded presentation. My preference, however, is to create a conversation with the client, learning as much about them as possible. Here's a guide that has been successful for me:

- Read the client. Take cues from what the client says and does to determine whether to make small talk or get right down to business.

- Listen for understanding. Read between the lines.

- Ask pertinent, thought-provoking questions. Prepare a list of five to ten questions based on what you know about the situation. (Some samples are provided in the next section.)

- Address all meeting attendees by name. Follow your client's lead about whether to use a title or first name or surname.

- Exude self-confidence without arrogance.

- Project a professional image with a firm handshake, appropriate attire, high-quality materials, and a genuine interest in the client.

What to Ask Potential Clients

General Questions

- What does your company [division, department] value most?

- What are your company's [division's, department's] vision and mission?

- What is your strategy to achieve your vision and mission?

- What are your company's [division's, department's, leadership team's] strengths?

- What is going well for your company [division, department, team]?

- What are the greatest challenges you will face over the next two years?

- What challenges do you need to overcome to meet your goals [objectives, mission]?

- Where is the greatest need for improvement?

- What prevents you from making that improvement?

- Describe the communication process. How well does it work?

- What experience have you had working with consultants?

- If you had one message to give your president [CEO, board, manager], what would it be?

- What should I have asked but didn't?

Questions Specific to the Situation

- Why are you considering this project?

- Can you define the scope of this project?

- How will you know that you have gotten a return on the investment for the money and time you will spend on it?

- What will be different as a result of this project?

- What behavioral changes do you expect when this project is successful?

- What specific improvements and changes would you like to see occur?

- What obstacles to success can you predict?

- How will you be involved in this project?

- How will a decision be made about proceeding with this project?

- What's the next step? Do you want a proposal?

Follow Up After Every Meeting

Get in the habit of following up every meeting with a written note thanking the prospects for their time. Even if you will submit a proposal, dash off a quick note to maintain the momentum of a positive meeting.

Remember that you are still in the exploratory mode. Learn as much as you can at this stage about potential clients, your selling skills, and what you can do better next time.

This chapter helped you determine a need and analyze your competition to land your first work. You have just experienced your first marketing activities. Chapter Nine will expand your market planning.

Quick Start LISTS

Actions I Will Take

Ideas I Have

Questions I Have

Marketing

9

In this chapter you will

- Create a marketing plan
- Explore creative marketing options on a shoestring budget
- Practice a step-by-step process to write a client proposal
- Develop a client tracking system

What Marketing Is

Marketing is how you advertise, publicize, or otherwise inform others of your consulting services and products. Your goal is reached when clients purchase your services and products. You may be the best consultant in the world, but until others know about you and can purchase what you have to offer, you will not have any business. Obviously you cannot just sit back with your stack of business cards and wait for the phone to ring. You must market your products and services. You must promote yourself.

Your first work may be work that your former employer asked you to complete when you left to begin your consulting business. It may be work that you obtained through members of your network. But you will not be able to depend on people you know to keep you in business. You must reach out to others. The reaching out is your marketing, and your marketing plan will help identify and organize how you will accomplish that.

In Chapter Eight you identified your niche. Your niche focuses on two things important to your marketing plan. First, it identifies what range of products and services you provide. In other words, are you a generalist or a specialist? Second, it identifies the range of clients you serve. Do you serve a wide market or a narrow market? With this start, you can begin to develop a very simple marketing plan. Volumes and volumes have been written about marketing.

The ABCs of Marketing

Although lots has been written about marketing, it can be as easy as ABC:

- Assess your situation.
- Build a client base.
- Contact potential clients.

Assess Your Situation

You started this step in Chapter Eight by examining your consulting business from an internal and external (clients and competition) perspective. When developing a marketing plan, you will explore the discussion about what you offer and to whom in more depth.

A marketing plan requires that you determine where you are today, where you want to be, and what the gap is between these two. For example, you may be offering team-building seminars in which you follow up with coaching to senior leaders. What you really want to be doing is increasing your coaching services and eliminating the team-building seminars. Your marketing plan will take this into consideration and create a road map to that end.

When you explore your customer base, you may discover that 85 percent of your revenues come from government clients. Since they pay lower fees than your private industry clients, you may develop a plan to increase the percentage of private industry clients. And of course you should always be aware of what your competition is doing. Creating a marketing plan, however, requires you to dedicate time to a more thorough examination.

Build a Client Base

Once you have assessed your situation, you will use the information to create a marketing plan that targets specific clients or groups of clients. You cannot pursue every potential client, so you need to make difficult decisions in narrowing your client base.

You will place everything into the mix that you have learned in the "A" step about you and your business, your current and potential clients, and your competitors, and look for opportunities. This step will help you identify advertising and publicity options to consider, the marketing media you will use, which clients to target, and what your budget will be.

Contact Potential Clients

This third step, the "C," is actually the follow-through with regard to your marketing plan. This is the sales part of the marketing process.

A marketing plan is a failure if sales do not result. And for consultants, there is only one time to market: all the time. You are on and marketing no matter where you are or what you are doing.

Quick ··········▶ **TIP**

Marketing is a fascinating subject and critical to your success. If you want to learn more about marketing, contact your local community college, and register for a course. You will not only learn about the marketing basics, but you will also be exposed to ideas you will be able to translate to your consulting business. You might also consider buying my book *Marketing Your Consulting Services*. It is jam-packed with a bundle of ideas that work.

Create Your Marketing Plan

This section walks you through the ABCs of marketing to create your first marketing plan.

Your marketing plan must be in writing. A written plan puts discipline into your ideas, enables you to measure success, and provides data for future use.

In Chapter Five you developed a business plan, and one of its sections was devoted to a marketing plan. You can use that information now to flesh out the marketing plan.

Review the eight steps presented here. Then use the questions in the next section to build your marketing plan. You will use the information to complete your first annual marketing plan. Have fun! Marketing can be almost as much fun as consulting.

Step 1: Analyze the Present

Market research should be an ongoing activity, so create a systematic method to keep information on client needs up-to-date. If you conduct training as part of your consulting, you can easily gather data through evaluations at the end of the training session. Other methods you might consider are mailed questionnaires, telephone surveys, electronic surveys, or face-to-face interviews.

You want to know how you are perceived in the marketplace, whether you meet your clients' expectations, whether you project the image you desire, and whether you have the reputation you desire.

If you have been in business for over a year, complete this analysis by calling several of your clients to obtain information. For absolutely honest feedback, you will have to conduct anonymous research. If you are just starting out, analyze what you expect to happen over the next twelve months.

Step 2: Clarify Your Strategy

Clarify where your business is heading. You have created your niche in lots of detail. Examine what you stated as your niche in Chapter Eight.

Here you will describe your targeted client base and what you will offer them.

Step 3: Set Measurable Six- to Twelve-Month Goals

You know the value of goal setting. Set your goals here. Be specific, and write them so that they are measurable. Add time limits to them so you can tell whether you accomplished your goals in a timely manner. Your goals should be results oriented, not activity based. Here are some examples:

- Generate $400,000 in new business from July 1 to January 3.
- Acquire three new clients by February 28.
- Acquire one new client in the banking industry by February 28.
- Present at one new conference in the next calendar year

Step 4: Select Marketing Tactics to Accomplish Your Goals

Tactics are actions you will take to get the word out that you are in business. Marketing experts often divide these tactics into a number of categories. Sometimes marketing is divided into direct and indirect marketing methods. Direct methods include things such as telemarketing, direct mail, magazine advertising, and directory advertising. Indirect marketing methods include such activities as public speaking, seminars, professional affiliations, writing books and articles, public relations, and newsletters.

Marketing is also divided into advertising and promotion. The differentiation by some is that advertising is paid for and promotion is free. All of these items qualify as ways to get the word out.

We are not going to concern ourselves about whether your tactics are direct or indirect, advertising or promotion, or any other category. You just need to begin to think about actions you will take to get the word out. Examples include the following:

- Make twenty-five contacts in the banking industry.
- Submit proposals to at least three new conferences.
- Submit an article to *Banking Today*.

Step 5: Identify Resources

There is always a cost to marketing, whether you take out a four-color full-page ad in a professional journal or write a letter to the editor in your local paper. The ad may cost $10,000 and little of your time if you hire a marketing firm to develop it.

The letter may be less than a dollar for a stamp, paper, and an envelope, but six hours of your time to craft it. You must weigh the cost and the benefits to determine whether the investment makes sense to you. How many people will see the ad? How many will see the letter? How many of these people will be members of your niche market? What are the chances of one person responding to your action?

Besides time and money, your resources could also be people. If you are targeting a specific industry, for example, you could have a booth at the industry's conference, take an ad out in its journal, or take someone you know in the industry to lunch to brainstorm ideas for approaching organizations within the industry.

Step 6: Develop an Annual Marketing Activity Calendar

Your marketing activities will be more appealing if you break them down into smaller steps. For example, if your goal is to have one new client in a particular industry within the next six months, the steps to reach that goal might look something like this:

- Ask Wisconsin staff to help identify ten possible clients by July 5.
- Gather information about the organizations by July 15.
- Brainstorm potential mailing content with Katrina.
- Send first mailing by August 5.
- Complete follow-up calls by August 15.
- Send follow-up mailing with article by September 5.
- Arrange meetings by October 5.

A layout for your marketing calendar is provided in the next section.

Step 7: Implement Your Plan

If you have developed your plan, you need to be faithful about implementing it. Don't get behind. Even when you're too busy to market, you must market. There will be times when you are busy with a big project and your desire will be to complete the project and skip the marketing. The problem is that when the big project is completed, you may not have another project to be busy with! The time to market is all the time. And the most important time to market is when you are too busy to market.

Step 8: Monitor Your Results and Adjust as Needed

Your plan is your best guess at the moment. You may need to adjust it as changes occur, perhaps in the economy or in the industry you have targeted. Perhaps you targeted small nonprofits and realize that their decision-making process is too long for you. Therefore, you may need to add some larger for-profits to your mix to decrease the gaps you have between projects.

Whatever is happening, you will use this information as input to the analysis you conduct for your plan next year.

Build Your Marketing Plan

Take some time now to develop a marketing plan for your business.

Step 1: Analyze the Present

How are you perceived in the marketplace?

How do you compare to your competition?

What's happening to your revenue and profits?

How satisfied are your customers?

How do your customers describe you and your performance?

How pleased are you with your image in the marketplace?

Step 2: Clarify Your Strategy

Return to Chapter Eight and review your niche. What strategy will you use to meet those goals?

Describe your targeted client base:

Identify at least seven ways you could reach these clients:

1.

2.

3.

4.

5.

6.

7.

Describe what you will offer these clients:

Identify at least seven things you could tell your clients about these services:

1.

2.

3.

4.

5.

6.

7.

Step 3: Set Measurable Six- to Twelve-Month Goals

Set at least five measurable goals to build your business (remember to focus on the niche you have described):

1.

2.

3.

4.

5.

Are all five goals measurable?

Have you attached a time to each goal?

Step 4: Select Marketing Tactics to Accomplish Your Goals

You have hundreds of possibilities. Here's a list of nouns to start your creative juices flowing:

business cards	letters	seminars	television
speeches	brochures	conferences	articles
clubs	postcards	network	lunch
e-mail	Internet, Podcast	directories	news releases
mailings	trade shows	ads	telephone calls
friends	past bosses	books	newsletters
associations	journals	direct mail	logos
stunts	greeting cards	telemarketing	civic organizations
competitors	church	community	press releases
radio	newspapers	college parties	pictures
celebrations	congratulation notes	free presentations	testimonials
charity	rumors	holidays	
audiotapes	interviews	awards	

Use these nouns to create at least twenty actions that you could complete that will put your name in front of the potential clients you've targeted. Each has many possibilities. For interviews, you could interview twenty industry leaders and publish the results; you could interview a well-respected person at a conference; you could be interviewed by a newspaper about your specialty; you could interview a university professor and send a transcript or a CD (with permission of course) to potential clients; you could interview your clients' customers and include the information in your proposal.

Now it's your turn. Consider all of the possibilities, and make up your own. Then decide on at least fifteen that are a fit for your clients, your budget, and your personality.

1.

2.

3.

4.

5.

6.

7.

8.

9.

10.

11.

12.

13.

14.

15.

16.

17.

18.

19.

20.

Step 5: Identify Resources

What resources will it take to produce your marketing tactics? Select six of your
tactics and estimate how much time and money will be required and who will help
you complete your actions.

	Tactic	Who Will Help	Time	Cost
1.				
2.				
3.				
4.				
5.				
6.				

Step 6: Develop an Annual Marketing Activity Calendar

Lay out your plan for the year on the Annual Marketing Activity form.

Annual Marketing Activity

Marketing Activity for (Year)	Jan	Feb	Mar	April	May	June	July	Aug	Sept	Oct	Nov	Dec
Dates												
Cost												
Total Budgeted Costs												

Source: Biech, *The Business of Consulting,* 2nd ed., 2007.

Step 7: Implement Your Plan

How will you ensure that you complete everything on your calendar every month?

How will you reward yourself for completing your marketing activities?

Quick TIP

Would you like to have your marketing plan developed for free? Most business schools require marketing students to develop a marketing plan. You could be the recipient. Contact your local college's business school to learn who the marketing instructors are. Then contact them. To ensure that this is not only free but also valuable, do two things. First, allow enough time. It will be a long process, usually occurring over almost a full semester. Second, stay involved. Your input will be critical to provide correct data. Your involvement will more than likely increase the enthusiasm of the student. A side benefit may be getting feedback from the professor.

Step 8: Monitor Your Results and Adjust as Needed

How will you track your results?

How will you know if you need to adjust your plans?

Marketing on a Shoestring Budget

Start-up costs are always more than most of us can predict. What are some ideas for marketing when your revenues are less than you would like?

The process that yields the best results dollar for dollar has already been presented to you. Return to Chapter Eight, and review the nine-step plan for landing your first clients. That plan has worked over and over for me. Here are some other ideas:

- If you are planning to attend a conference, submit a proposal to speak. Often the conference sponsor will pay your registration if you speak.

- Make certain you always project a high-quality image through your stationery, business cards, and the letters you write. Cheap cards or sloppy letters may cost much more than expensive stationery.

- Cards, letters, and telephone calls cost little as compared to an ad in a journal or the newspaper, and they can be personalized. Quite honestly, save your money—my experience has been that ads in journals, newspapers, or the yellow pages don't pull their weight in customers.

- Look for listings in consulting directories that are free or low cost.

- Pass out business cards freely. They are a great bargain, so be sure you have taken the time to word them perfectly and to get the perfect look.

- Offer to speak to civic organizations, and be sure to take your business cards with you.

- Do such a great job that your clients market for you.

For 113 other marketing ideas, see the list beginning on page 114 in the second edition of *The Business of Consulting*.

What About a Web Site?

Web sites are almost as common as a telephone number these days. And you can locate people everywhere who are willing to help you design your site. When marketing, you will often be asked, "Do you have a Web site?" If you do, it provides people with an easy way to get information about you and your consulting business.

To be sure your Web site projects your preferred image, hire a highly qualified Web designer to assist you. Review other Web sites the individual has designed, and be sure the person is a good communicator. Sometimes you will not know exactly what you want until you see a proposal. A good designer, that is, one who listens well, will be able to interpret what you want into a Web site that represents you and your consulting business accurately.

Ask for references, and establish a range of the design cost as well as what features that design will encompass. The initial design may be between two thousand and ten thousand dollars, depending on how many bells and whistles you want to include.

Your Web site should be effective but simple. Don't allow the designer to make it so complex that it takes a long time to download. Be sure it is easy to maneuver and to locate information that is important to clients and potential clients. There is always an urge to do something creative and different, and I applaud you for that. But take care that your Web site is not so different from others that your clients have difficulty finding the information that they need. You don't want one of their first experiences with you to be frustrating!

Develop a Web site with which people can interact by including a quiz, a self-assessment, or a puzzle. Customize the site to meet the needs of clients who might visit. Ask yourself, "What would potential clients be likely to want to find on my Web site?" Begin with a page that defines your company and the kind of work you do. You may wish to add a client list, samples of your materials, or a descriptive list of services and products you provide. Ensure that potential clients can e-mail you while visiting your site and ask your designer how you could capture names of interested visitors for follow-up.

Many people forget that individuals sometimes go to a Web site to find other ways to contact people or to determine where a business is located. Therefore, don't forget to include a telephone number, the address where your business is located, and its mail addresses if it is different from the street address.

Select a URL for the Web site that is easy to remember and makes sense to potential clients. Using your corporate name is the easiest.

Once you have a Web page, print the address on your business cards, stationery, pamphlets, and anywhere else it will be useful. Remember that the Internet is not intended to broadcast your message like other marketing media. Instead, you need to publish your Web site address so clients can find you and your information.

Finally, maintain your Web site regularly. Visit it often and respond to e-mails and other requests within twenty-four hours. If you have a calendar posted, keep it up to date and refresh your Web site every month or two.

Quick • • • • • • • • • • • • • • • • • • • ▶ **TIP**

Launching your Web site is a perfect excuse to contact your clients and market to them. Once your site is up and all the bugs are worked out, contact your clients and potential clients to obtain feedback about the site.

Write Winning Proposals

Proposals will become an integral part of your business development strategy. A proposal may be the last step in the sales process—a statement that summarizes how you have defined and clarified your prospective client's needs. At other times, it may be the first step in a bidding or an introductory process. In either case, it takes time to write a good proposal.

The secret to writing winning proposals is to listen carefully to the client and take good notes or, in the case of a Request for Proposal (RFP), read the information carefully and highlight important information. Give the speaker or the writer back exactly what is asked for. If they ask for a "corrective measures" design and you know that they mean "progressive discipline," use their words anyway. It is amazing to me how many people speak their own language in a proposal instead of the language that the client uses. Maybe your words are more descriptive or more appropriate, but if the client must translate your proposal before making a decision, your proposal will be near the bottom of the stack. Use their words, and you will be surprised at how often you hear clients say, "How did you know? That's exactly what we need!"

Steps to Writing a Proposal

A proposal is simply a statement of who will do what by when and for how much. Follow these steps when writing a proposal:

1. Gather as much information as you can before beginning to write. You might use the questions in Chapter Eight ("What to Ask Potential Clients") to gather some of the data.

2. Plan a structure that will be easy for your clients to find their way around. You may develop your own proposal structure, but the one that is presented here will serve you well. It includes a purpose statement, a description of the situation, a proposed approach, a time line, your qualifications, and the investment (cost) required to complete the plan.

3. Complete each section writing from your client's perspective, using your client's words and language. Be certain your writing is clear, concise, and descriptive.

4. If the RFP allows it, stay in touch with the client. Sometimes if the RFP is competitive, as is the case in many government RFPs, you are not allowed to speak to the client. If that is not the case, you can clarify information to avoid making assumptions, gather information you may have missed in earlier conversations, or test any creative options. Certainly you would not want to call every day and make a pest of yourself. Nevertheless, staying in touch, done well, can help to maintain rapport and confirm that you care and want to do a good job.

5. Have someone read your proposal to check for typos, clarity, accuracy, and understanding.

6. Print the proposal on the best paper that you have. Attach any supplemental material, add a cover to the front, place it in a folder, and either hand-deliver it or send it in an overnight package.

Writing the Proposal

Return to one of the clients you met with in Chapter Eight, and write your first proposal. Use the following guidelines to begin to sketch out your answers and information here.

Cover Page. Include the name of the proposal ("A Proposal Prepared for [Company Name]"), the date, your company name, and contact information.

Purpose Statement. Open with a statement something like this fill-in-the-blank model:

"This proposal is submitted at the request of **(name)**, **(title)**, **(company)**."
It includes a description of the situation, a suggested approach, a time line, and the expected investment for the effort.

Write your purpose statement in the space provided:

Description of the situation. Discuss the situation as it currently exists. You may include the current problem, the current need, the desire for the future, or any other pertinent data. Note here some of the specifics of the situation you might include in the proposal:

A proposed approach. This is where you describe exactly what you will do to accomplish the task. What is special about your approach? To make this section easier to understand, you may divide it into subsections and present them in the order that they will occur—for example, Data Gathering, Design, Content, Implementation, and Follow-Up. Make some notes about what you might include:

Time line. A time line is exactly what it sounds like. You will need to determine the level of detail you will include. It is always good to include specific dates. You can just list the dates down the left side and the tasks next to the dates. You may also present this information as a graphic picture.

Your qualifications. This is optional. You may choose to include a paragraph about why you are uniquely qualified to complete this project. You may also choose to attach a biographical sketch or your résumé, whichever is appropriate for the industry.

Investment and responsibilities. Use the word *investment* instead of *price* or *cost*. It will help your clients focus on your proposals as something that will benefit them rather than just "cost" them. I also include some of the key responsibilities required to complete the plan in this section. When tied to the investment, it makes an impressive package that says, "Look at all you're getting!" Responsibilities might include materials you will supply and actual work you will complete, such as interviews, specific sessions you will lead, and so on. State travel arrangements also. List the investment and responsibilities for your proposal here:

I close in this way:

> Your investment for (name of consultation) will be ($). In addition, travel will be billed at cost.

> The terms of this proposal are effective through (date).

> Executive-level references are available.

Attachments. Attachments may be included as an appendix to your proposal. They should be added only if they enhance the proposal. Attachments could include any or all of these items:

- Biographical sketches of the individuals who will work on the project

- A description of your company

- A client list

- Any related materials

Now turn to your computer and begin to enter a draft of your first proposal.

A proposal can also be written in a letter format. If you do that, it will be shorter and perhaps less formal. Use a formal letter format, with subheads within the letter's body. You can find a sample proposal in this format on page 138 in the book I coauthored with Linda B. Swindling, *The Consultant's Legal Guide.*

Keep a file of all your proposals. You'll be surprised to see the quality in each improve. In the future, you may even be able to use sections from one proposal for another.

Track Your Clients

"Track my clients?" you might be asking, "Why? I don't have any yet!" But you will! And with all the balls you will need to keep in the air, it's never too soon. Start tracking clients with the first contact you make. You will be surprised at how easily you forget what one client said or when you promised to follow up with a telephone call.

Completing the eight-step marketing plan in this chapter ensures that you have thought through how you will get the word out about your services. It will help you stay focused and committed to ongoing marketing of your services.

Quick  **TIP**

Make copies of the Client Contact Log, and place them next to your telephone or in a file folder. If you have a tendency toward a messy desk, copy the pages on canary yellow or some other bright color or file them in a brightly colored folder.

Client Contact Log

Organization/ Phone Number	Contact Person	Date	First Contact	Follow-Up	Date	Second Contact	Follow-Up	Date	Third Contact	Follow-Up

Source: The Consultant's Quick Start Guide: An Action Plan for Your First Year in Business, Second Edition. Copyright 2009 by John Wiley & Sons, Inc. Reproduced by permission of Pfeiffer, an Imprint of Wiley. www.pfeiffer.com (originally from Biech, 2007).

Tips to Become a Better Marketer

Remember that your business depends on your ability to continually bring in new business. Here are a few tips to become better at marketing. Attend to those that make sense for you.

- Learn to spot an opportunity when you hear it. Then grab it with gusto, and do something about it!

- Before you call on a prospective client, obtain a copy of the organizational chart listing all key people, and learn something about the organization's history and current culture.

- Develop name recognition within your industry by speaking at conferences, writing articles, and volunteering for your professional organization.

- Listen, listen, listen. Listen to what your potential clients say as well as what they do not say during a marketing call.

- Stay in touch with people as they move from one job to another, and turn reconnecting into a marketing opportunity.

- Develop relationships with those people whom you believe will be the next leaders of the organization.

- Market all the time. Make marketing a mind-set.

- Buy and read my book *Marketing Your Consulting Services* for hundreds of other ideas as practical as these.

Quick Start LISTS

Actions I Will Take

Ideas I Have

Questions I Have

Surviving the First Year

In this chapter you will

- Identify a plan to take care of your mental and physical health
- Establish a plan to manage your time
- Establish good habits for managing a business
- Establish a plan to balance your life
- Develop a personal ethics statement for operating your business

Take Care of Your Health

Many people I meet think of consulting as an exciting, high-powered career: flying from coast to coast, meeting with publishers in San Francisco and executives in New York City, staying at the Madison in Washington, D.C., or the Ritz Carlton in Dallas, eating at a coffee shop in Seattle. I am paid well, dress well, land large contracts, and hobnob with the influential. But that's only the first layer.

My friends know what my life is really like: up at 4:00 A.M. to catch a flight for a noon meeting, spending six hours in an airport because of delayed flights, canceling dinner plans, and finally arriving home at midnight. It is also about eating poorly prepared restaurant food, writing proposals until the wee hours of the morning, and losing a contract due to a technicality. Most of all, it is about long hours.

You do have the freedom to set your own schedule—but often those hours are long. You will make enough money to eat well. And it will take a concerted effort to do so when you're on the road.

Identify how you will continue to maintain a healthy lifestyle by answering these questions:

What was your exercise routine before becoming a consultant (or, What is the ideal exercise routine you'd like to start)? How will you ensure that you get regular exercise?

What eating habits do you want to maintain? What new eating habits do you want to start? How will you do this while traveling?

What kinds of things have caused stress for you in the past? What stress reducers have you used that work? What is your plan to prevent stress as a consultant?

Manage Your Time

We all have exactly twenty-four hours in every day. And while we all talk about saving time, we really cannot. Time continues to march on. We can't save it. We can, however, shave time. Here are some time-shaving tips for you. Then we'll explore your greatest time waster.

The Big Jobs

Work on several large projects rather than dozens of small projects. You use a great deal of time traveling from one client to another, remembering names, and getting up to speed on the project. This means that you must use a marketing strategy that ensures that you acquire larger projects rather than smaller ones.

Invoice Ease

Keep an invoice format on your computer for clients who will incur repeat billings. When it's time to bill them, simply complete the date and the invoice amount and print it out.

Tickler Files

Keep tickler files by month in your desk drawer or on your computer desktop. Place items in them that need attention in each particular month. When you pull the file for each month, you will be reminded of what needs to be completed. For example, when I pull the May file, I have written items under both personal and business. Personal: Annual checkup, call to initiate lawn mowing, and clean air conditioner. Business: Renew lease, submit corporation minutes, and pay ASTD dues. On the inside of that folder I also have a list of everyone I know who has a birthday in May.

As you continue to consult, you will acquire your own time shavers. To truly identify how you spend your time, you will need to keep a Time Management Log, like the one shown here. The log will give you the data you need to identify where you could manage your time better. Keep the log for a week or two. You may be very surprised at where your time goes.

For example, the last time I kept a time log, I was surprised to learn that when I am in the office, I spend almost half of my time on the telephone, either talking or calling and leaving messages for people who aren't available. Related to this, I found that waiting for someone to return my call was delaying the start of some projects. Was it any wonder that I could not get proposals written while I was in the office? I initiated two things as a result of reviewing this information. First, I work out of my home office when I have large projects such as proposals or writing a book. Second, I have my staff tell people when I will be available for phone calls—Thursday between 10:00 A.M. and noon, for example. It has shaved quite a bit of time for me and I am able to do my priorities in a more timely manner.

Time-Management Log

| Name: _____ | Date: _____ |

Hour	15-Minute Intervals				Daily Summaries
12:00 am					List task categories after each
1:00 am					letter code (meetings, telephone
2:00 am					calls, marketing, consulting,
3:00 am					administration, planning, and so
4:00 am					forth). Then put the correspond-
5:00 am					ing letter into the block that was
6:00 am					dominated by each task. Do not
7:00 am					allow more than one hour to pass
8:00 am					before updating this log. Multiply
9:00 am					the number of blocks by 15 min-
10:00 am					utes to find out how much time
11:00 am					was spent on each task.
12:00 pm					

Daily Summaries

List task categories after each letter code (meetings, telephone calls, marketing, consulting, administration, planning, and so forth). Then put the corresponding letter into the block that was dominated by each task. Do not allow more than one hour to pass before updating this log. Multiply the number of blocks by 15 minutes to find out how much time was spent on each task.

Code	Task	#		Total Time
A.	_____	____	× 15 =	_____
B.	_____	____	× 15 =	_____
C.	_____	____	× 15 =	_____
D.	_____	____	× 15 =	_____
E.	_____	____	× 15 =	_____
F.	_____	____	× 15 =	_____
G.	_____	____	× 15 =	_____
H.	_____	____	× 15 =	_____
I.	_____	____	× 15 =	_____
J.	_____	____	× 15 =	_____

Hour
1:00 pm
2:00 pm
3:00 pm
4:00 pm
5:00 pm
6:00 pm
7:00 pm
8:00 pm
9:00 pm
10:00 pm
11:00 pm

Source: The Consultant's Quick Start Guide: An Action Plan for Your First Year in Business, Second Edition. Copyright 2009 by John Wiley & Sons, Inc. Reproduced by permission of Pfeiffer, an Imprint of Wiley. www.pfeiffer.com (originally from Biech, 2007).

Looking for more time? You'll never find time for everything. You must make it. The following list of time management techniques will not be new to you. But remind yourself of those that you could practice more diligently. Check the box next to the ones you could do better:

❏ Set your priorities first thing in the morning or the last thing at night for the next day.

❏ Do your top A priorities first.

❏ Tackle large projects in stages.

❏ Identify your best times, that is, your best time for writing, best time to make telephone calls, and so forth.

❏ Use your waiting and travel time productively: make lists, listen to tapes, balance your checkbook.

❏ Carry notecards or a small notebook to list ideas or reminders.

❏ Handle each piece of paper only once.

❏ Have a place for everything.

❏ Set deadlines.

❏ Make decisions in a timely way. Indecision is a time thief.

❏ Always ask, "Is this the best use of my time right now?"

❏ Set a schedule, and stick to it.

❏ Take short breaks often.

❏ Have something to do when you're put on hold.

❏ Become a great communicator.

❏ Minimize interruptions.

As a business owner, time is your most precious resource. Manage it well, and guard it jealously. Once it is gone, you will never get it back.

Before you leave this section, pull out your day planner or calendar, and do a quick assessment on how you have spent your time so far this week. What does it tell you? Are you doing the things that will get you to the goals you identified in Chapter Two? What changes might you make? Do you have any bad habits that will be difficult to overcome? For example, do you like to talk on the phone, do you spend more time with the daily crossword puzzle in the morning than you want, or do you procrastinate when faced with big projects?

Establish Good Habits

What better time to start new habits—good habits—than when starting a business? Good habits will make your business run more smoothly, ensuring you are making the best use of your time. They may seem like little things, but they will turn up as critical sooner or later. New habits can begin when you want them to begin. Here are a few that are worth starting now:

- Create a good filing system. Chapter Seven addressed the good filing habits you could initiate. Go back to that chapter, and review them before reading about other good habits.

- Add copyrights to all original documents. More than once I've found my original work floating around in an organization or being used by another consultant. I have always been willing to share, but I like to be asked. If I have put my copyright on something, I know there was some effort expended in cutting it off, whiting it out, or taping over it. If your integrity is ever questioned, a dated copyright on your material protects you and your work.

- Bill all completed work immediately. One of the best favors you can do for your cash flow is to send the invoice to your client within twenty-four hours of completing the project. Your bank statement will thank you.

- Make follow-up with clients your top priority. Seems logical, doesn't it? You will be surprised at how many things can come between you and a simple return telephone call. Time gets away from me in the afternoon. All too soon it's 3:30, whoops! 4:30 on the East Coast—too late to return that call. Don't let it happen.

- Date everything. Someday you will look through a file, find just what you wanted, and pat yourself on the back for a good filing system, only to find out that the survey was dated August—that's it. Just "August." August what? The most important number has been left off. It's happened to me many more times than I care to mention.

What good habits do you want to start with this business? List them here:

Balance Your Life

One of the most challenging aspects of being a consultant is finding balance. While I do not profess to have the answer, I do have some suggestions to offer.

Identify Any Imbalance

Identify what seems to be out of balance in your life. How do you know? Geoff Bellman, author of *The Consultant's Calling* (2002), uses this exercise in his sessions. List three things you value most in your life. Write them here:

1.

2.

3.

Now scan your checkbook and your calendar. Do your checkbook and calendar indicate that those are the most valuable things in your life? If not, determine what you can do about it. Write your ideas here.

Make Your Own Rules

Make up rules that help you maintain your balance. Create rules that help put your business in perspective. Tell yourself, "If it's not done by 6:00 P.M., it can wait until tomorrow." I sometimes spend too much time fretting about a decision on the horizon that won't occur for days, weeks, or months. I have learned to put it out of my mind by setting a date with myself: "I'll think about that on November 13," and then I do. Perhaps your rule is, "My number one business rule is to spend Saturday morning with my children."

What rules can you make to help you add more balance to your life? List two here:

1.

2.

Enjoy the Doing

Don't overload yourself so much that you miss the fun in the doing. If you like consulting, enjoy all of it. Much of the pleasure is in the doing.

Are you enjoying what you are doing? How will you ensure that you enjoy all of it?

Take Time Off

It's important to take a break from your business. Go on a vacation. Go to a day spa. Spend an afternoon reading a book. Visit a state park. Take your niece on a picnic. Go for a walk around the block.

How do you plan to take time off this year?

Identify Other Interests

Join an investment club. Learn golf. Try embroidery. Fly a kite. Collect something. Visit an antique store. Go hiking. Read catalogues. Learn to paint. Take a gourmet cooking class. Write poetry. Work crossword puzzles. Refurbish a classic car. Study your heritage. Go for walks. Develop your family tree. Write a letter. Plan a trip with your spouse, your children, your parents, or a friend.

List five things here you've always wanted to try.

1.

2.

3.

4.

5.

Take Advantage of Being Your Own Boss

If you work at home, find ways and times to get away from it all. Go for a walk; work out at the gym a couple of days each week; eat lunch in your backyard. If you work in an office, stay home a couple of days each month and work on your deck.

How can you take advantage of being your own boss?

Manage Your Balance

Issues of balance are more acute during transitions. So if you are going through your transition to consulting, you should know what to expect.

How might balance shift initially in the various areas of your life, and what do you want to do to maintain balance?

Social?

Family?

Spiritual?

Business?

Education?

Others?

In some respects, the issue of balance in life is one of time management. You must prioritize deliberately, based on what you want out of life—what you value.

Did You Hear the One About the Consultant . . . ?
Developing a Personal Ethics Statement

These days there are almost as many consultant jokes as lawyer jokes. As a consultant, your principles are always on the line. What do you stand for?

Begin to identify a list of the ethical standards you will uphold as a consultant. This list will grow as your business grows. Your ethics should be those things you feel deeply about and believe are the foundation of who you are.

You might create ethical statements around some of the following:

- Kinds of projects you will accept

- How you use your time

- The quality of your work

- Kinds of organizations you will work with

- Delivery of services

- How you treat your clients

- Continuous improvement issues

- Goals for your clients

- Work standards

- Pricing

- How you deal with expenses

- Anything else you feel strongly about

Begin your statement of ethics here. Transfer it to a place where you will see it regularly. Update it as you and your business grow.

Although this book focuses on developing a consulting practice, you must be certain to work toward a balanced life as well.

Quick Start LISTS

Actions I Will Take

Ideas I Have

Questions I Have

So, Now What? Year Two and Beyond

In this chapter you will

- Assess your progress
- Plan your next steps

Assess Your Progress

Congratulations! You've made it though your first year of consulting. And if you are reading this chapter, you must be considering moving forward. Great!

Let's assess your progress and plan your next steps. Take some time to answer the following questions, which address your first year in consulting.

Is consulting all that you had dreamed it would be? Why or why not?

How satisfied do you think your clients are? How do you know?

How successful have you been financially?

How much fun are you having?

Now compare your responses to some of these thoughts:

Is consulting all that you dreamed it would be? People often see consulting as a dream job. You most likely have learned the realities of the business. Travel isn't as glamorous as it first appears. Working at home without someone to talk to gets lonely, and clients who don't pay their bills in a timely manner can wreak havoc on your savings account. All in all, though, it is a great way to make a living. You have freedom and flexibility to do it your way. Your first year is always the most difficult. There is so much to learn! I hope you made some money and had some fun too.

How satisfied do you think your clients are? How do you know? If this is to continue to be your profession, you need lots of very satisfied customers who will continue to use you, will recommend you to other clients, and will sing your praises. You have probably had conversations with many of them asking about your services and what you could do better. Stay in touch with all of these clients. Create mailing lists—electronic, as well as a postal mail list—so that you can run labels easily to keep them informed of what you are doing. These clients will be your customer base for the rest of the time you are in business. Some will use you again and again. Some will refer you over and over to many others.

How successful have you been financially? How are you doing? You should be able to begin to pay back some of those loans you took out during year one. If not, it might be time to take a hard look at your numbers. Are expenses higher than you anticipated? Is that due to not having all the data for good estimates? Or are you being more extravagant than a start-up company should be? In either case, there is an important lesson for you. If expenses are not higher, is income lower than you projected? Why is that? How would you rate your marketing efforts? Are you marketing "all the time"? You need to make money to stay in business.

How much fun are you having? Or, as my friend Pam says, "Are we having fun yet?" Remember my comment in Chapter One: "We should not get up to go to work in the morning. We should be able to get up and go to play!" Consulting can be play. The transition to get there may be difficult for everyone involved. Are you still going through some of the transition trials? If so, do you see an end in sight? Are the people around you having fun too? Do you hear pride in their voices when they discuss what you are doing? Pay attention to that balance because it's critical. Is consulting as much fun as you expected?

Quick
Start

ACTION

Review Your First Year with Your Family

It's time to sit down and have a frank discussion with your spouse, significant other, roommate, or family. Right now, without hesitation, block out time on your calendar for that discussion. Use these questions to guide your discussion:

- How satisfied have we been with the past year's arrangements?
- What has worked well this past year?
- How would each of us rate the following?
    - Communication?
    - Financial situation?
    - Personal time?
    - Work time?
- What has been the most difficult change?
- How well have we adjusted to the office arrangements?
- What's been the most satisfying for each of us?
- How much fun are we all having?
- Have we had enough time together? Too much?
- What can we do better next year?
- How will we know it's better?

Plan Your Next Steps

Spend time thinking about your next steps. Let's examine them from your professional perspective, your financial perspective, and your personal perspective.

Professional

You will most likely learn more during your first year of consulting than at almost any other time in your life. This past year has also been a time that tested your capabilities as they have never been tested before. Go back and read Chapter One in this guide. You might be surprised at the new meaning that all of those words have now.

What do you still need to learn this year about running your business? Do you need to know more about organizing yourself and your office? If you knew more about marketing, would that task be more fun? How about finance? Are you as good at crunching those numbers and knowing what they are telling you? How about process improvement? Do you know how to determine the root cause when something goes wrong and address that to prevent it from occurring again? How are your administrative skills? Thinking about getting some help so that you can be more productive on other things? What is your plan for learning what you need?

You owe it to your clients to stay on top of all that is happening in the field. What did you do this past year to maintain your skills, knowledge, and expertise? What will you do next year? What professional organizations will you join? What professional journals will you read? What conferences will you attend?

How well have you maintained your network of professionals for support and growth? What can you do this next year to give your network a boost?

Financial

Take a good look at your numbers for the past year and determine the following:

- Was your income as high as you projected?
- Were your expenses at the level you projected?
- Did you have lots of highs and lows over the year?
- Were you able to pay yourself the salary you planned?

Profit

Profit is the reason businesses exist, and it doesn't just happen; you must plan for it. (Remember your business plan?) As a good business owner, you should plan to have more profits than if you simply put that same investment away and let it grow interest. How much is a good profit? Since you can probably make 10 percent interest by investing your money, that is a place to begin.

You should consider your first year in business a smashing success if you were able to pay yourself the salary you intended. Your second year, however, should find you planning for a profit. Your goal should be to pay yourself a good salary and in addition begin to have a 10 to 30 percent profit on top of that every year. Profit is what is left over after all the expenses are paid. You will pay taxes on that profit.

How do you begin to manage your business to increase profits? There are many things that go into the formula. To increase profits you can:

- Increase the number of billable days

- Increase the price of your services

- Decrease expenses

You also must consider the following:

- If you increase your price, will you continue to sell as much?

- How will your clients respond to a higher price?

- Could you increase quality or the value added for a client to justify a higher price?

- How do your prices compare now to your competitors' prices?

Review Your Niche

How did you do with your marketing this year? Could you have done more to get the word out about you and the services you offer? Perhaps you should broaden your niche. How could you do that? Here are some ways:

- You could broaden the services and products you offer to existing clients.

- You could attract new customers—perhaps broadening the customer base niche that you have defined.

- You could expand your line of products and services. Any of the following could become legitimate consulting profit centers:

  - Write a newsletter for profit (rather than as a marketing tool).

  - Sell CDs or DVDs of your presentations.

  - Write and sell a book, though my experience is that you must self-publish to truly make money.

  - Host public seminars.

  - Produce and sell directories.

  - Become a public speaker. Join the National Speakers Association (NSA) if this is one of your choices.

In the end, there are really only two things you can do differently to change your financial situation:

- Bring in more income.

- Allow fewer expenses.

But you have a multitude of ways to do both.

Although first-year businesses rarely produce a profit, you should plan for a profit during your second year. How will you increase profits next year?

Personal

How well have you taken care of yourself? How well did you take care of your mental and physical health? Were you able to get the same exercise that you enjoyed before you became a consultant? How's your stress level? Were you able to keep all the balls in the air and still feel sane? How's the diet? If you had a home office, were you able to resist the refrigerator? What are your plans for next year?

How did you do at managing your time? Only worked a few weekends? That's great. Did you take a family vacation this year? If not, are you planning one soon?

Have you been able to maintain a balance? Have you found time for friends, family, and hobbies, in addition to time for work? Would you change that balance if you could?

Have you enjoyed the benefits of being your own boss? Perhaps you were able to attend your daughter's first dance recital at three in the afternoon. Perhaps you were able to work ten to midnight when no one bothers you and sleep in the next day. Perhaps you've been able to read your professional journals in the neighborhood park. Perhaps you've been able to spend all afternoon reading business books and sipping coffee in your local bookstore. Can you take greater advantage of the benefits of being your own boss next year?

Have you seen how the financial gains can support you and your family? Did you provide all the benefits that you would have had if you were someone's employee? If not, this is the time to review them and decide what you want to do. Did your retirement contribution suffer because you were starting your business? Now is the time to boost that up.

Bring It All Together

I've presented several new directions for you to consider. How do you bring it all together? First go back to Chapter Two and examine your goals. Are you closer to your goals than you were a year ago? Have your goals changed? How will new or adjusted goals affect your consulting business? Explain here.

Assuming you will continue your consulting business, begin to complete the following questions and tasks. Check off each as you complete it:

☐ Review all of your financial statements. Examine your revenue projections for next year, your budget, and your expense records. What changes will you make for next year?

☐ Evaluate your cash flow situation. Do you bill immediately on completion of a project? Do your clients pay you in a timely manner? If this is less than satisfactory, develop a process that will increase the chances of their paying you faster. Describe the process you will use next year.

- [ ] Review your pricing structure. Should you charge more? Less? Should you have different levels of pricing for different clients? For different services? Should you expand your services or your products? Make a decision about your pricing structure for next year.

- [ ] Review your business plan. Although you should have referred to it regularly throughout the year, now study it more carefully. Are you wiser about your competition than you were last year? What do you still need to learn? Rate your progress on your goals. What new goals will you set for next year?

- [ ] Review your relationship with your accountant, attorney, banker, and insurance representative. Are you satisfied? What services would you like that you are not receiving? Is it time to meet with any of them to evaluate services? What changes do you want next year?

☐ Review your client relationships. Are your clients beginning to refer you to other clients? Have you completed all projects with high marks of satisfaction? If you had any difficulties, are you satisfied that you have dealt with the root cause to ensure it doesn't occur again? What will you do differently next year?

☐ Review your marketing plan. Did you achieve your goals? What will you change for next year? Will you increase your marketing budget? What clients can you tap for referrals? How will you market your business differently next year?

☐ Review the location of your office. Are you still satisfied? Running out of room? Wearing out your welcome at home? Is your business intruding on your home life? Is your home life intruding on your business? Is the image of working out of your house an issue for your clients? For you? If you move, how will you ensure a smooth transition? Where will your office be located next year?

☐ How about employees? Are you considering hiring them now? Who? To fulfill what roles? Where will they work? Where will you find them? When will you bring them in? Will they be full time or part time? Will they be employees or subcontractors? Be sure to check the Internal Revenue Service's independent contractor guidelines and discuss this with your attorney. How will you make this a reality next year?

☐ Look far out to five or ten years from now. What do you see yourself doing? How will your consulting practice look at that time? How and when will you leave the business? Sell it? Leave it to your child? Slip out the back door? What can you do next year to move in the direction of your future ten years from now?

☐ Did you take care of yourself this year? Remember that your business is nothing without you. You are the business. How well did you manage your time, deal with stress, take care of your health? How well did you balance your life? What will you do differently next year?

Quick
Start

ACTION

Review Your First Year with a Colleague

Contact a member of your network to schedule a time when this person will go over your responses with you. Ask for input about your answers for next year.

- -

This chapter has been a review of your progress to date. It should have given you reason to pause and consider what you did well, what needs improvement, and what you might do differently next year.

Consulting is a challenging yet rewarding profession. You will work harder than you ever have before, yet love the work more than any other. It can be risky, yet the payoffs are worth it.

If you've worked your way through this Quick Start Guide, you've "wished on paper," and now you have a plan!

Quick Start LISTS

Actions I Will Take

Ideas I Have

Questions I Have

Reading List

Bacal, R. (2002). *The complete idiot's guide to consulting.* Madison, WI: CWL Publishing Enterprises.

Baily, D., & Sproston, C. (1993). *Choosing and using training consultants.* Brookfield, VT: Gower.

Bell, C. R., & Nadler, L. (1979). *The client-consultant handbook.* Houston, TX: Gulf.

Bellman, G. M. (2002). *The consultant's calling* (2nd ed.). San Francisco: Jossey-Bass.

Bellman, G. M., Block, P., & Boehm, B. (1986). *Find the right consultant.* Alexandria, VA: ASTD.

Biech, E. (1995, Summer). Ten mistakes CEOs make about training. *William and Mary Business Review*, 13–16.

Biech, E. (2003). *Marketing your consulting services.* San Francisco: Pfeiffer.

Biech, E. (2007). *The business of consulting* (2nd ed.). San Francisco: Jossey-Bass/Pfeiffer.

Biech, E. (2007). *Ninety world-class activities by ninety world-class trainers.* San Francisco: Jossey-Bass/Pfeiffer.

Biech, E. (Ed.). (2007). *The Pfeiffer book of successful team-building tools* (2nd ed.). San Francisco: Jossey-Bass/Pfeiffer.

Biech, E. (2007). *A practical guide to change.* Alexandria, VA: ASTD Press.

Biech, E., & Swindling, L. B. (2000). *The consultant's legal guide.* San Francisco: Jossey-Bass/Pfeiffer.

Biswas, S., & Twitchelle, D. (2001). *Management consulting: A complete guide to the industry* (2nd ed.). Hoboken, NJ: Wiley.

Block, P. (2000). *Flawless consulting* (2nd ed.). San Francisco: Jossey-Bass/Pfeiffer.

Bond, W. J. (1997). *Going solo.* New York: McGraw-Hill.

Brown, P. C. (1994). *Jumping the job track.* New York: Crown.

Careers in management consulting 2006 ed.: WetFeet Insider Guide. San Francisco: WetFeet.

Carucci, R. A., & Tetenbaum, T. J. (2000). *The value-creating consultant: How to build and sustain lasting client relationships.* New York: AMACOM.

Chung, E. (2002). *Vault career guide to consulting: An indispensable guide to landing a consulting position and succeeding in a consulting career.* Boulder, CO: Vault.

Dinnocenzo, D. A. (1999). *101 tips for telecommuters.* San Francisco: Berrett-Koehler.

Florzak, D. (1999). *Successful independent consulting: Turn your career experience into a consulting business.* Brookfield, IL: Logical Directions.

Fox, J. (2000). *How to become a rainmaker.* New York: Hyperion.

Freedman, R. (2000). *The IT consultant: A commonsense framework for managing the client relationship.* San Francisco: Jossey-Bass/Pfeiffer.

Holtz, H. (1994). *The business plan guide for independent consultants.* Hoboken, NJ: Wiley.

Kintler, D., & Adams, B. (1998). *Streetwise independent consulting.* Holbrook, MA: Adams Media.

Koestenbaum, P. (2003). *The philosophic consultant: Revolutionizing organizations with ideas.* San Francisco: Jossey-Bass/Pfeiffer.

Lewin, M. D. (1995). *The overnight consultant.* Hoboken, NJ: Wiley.

Lewin, M. D. (1997). *The consultant's survival guide.* Hoboken, NJ: Wiley.

Lewis, L. (2000). *What to charge: Pricing strategies for freelancers and consultants.* Putnam Valley, NY: Aletheia Publications.

Moss, W. (2005). *Starting from scratch: Secrets from twenty-one ordinary people who made the entrepreneurial leap.* Chicago: Dearborn Trade Publishing.

Nelson, B., & Economy, P. (1997). *Consulting for dummies.* Hoboken, NJ: Wiley.

Phillips, J. (2000). *The consultant's scorecard: Tracking results and bottom-line impact of consulting projects.* New York: McGraw-Hill.

Phillips, J., & Phillips, P. (Eds.). (2002). *Building a successful consulting practice.* Alexandria, VA: ASTD Press.

Riddle, J. (2001). *Entrepreneur magazine's start-ups: Consulting business.* Irvine, CA: Entrepreneur Press.

Shefsky, L. E. (1994). *Entrepreneurs are made, not born.* New York: McGraw-Hill.

Silberman, M. (2001). *The consultant's tool kit.* New York: McGraw-Hill.

Stern, C. W., & Deimler, M. (2006). *The Boston Consulting Group on 2006 strategy: Classic concepts and new perspectives* (2nd ed.). Hoboken, NJ: Wiley.

Weiss, A. (2002). *Million dollar consulting: The professional's guide to growing a practice* (3rd ed.). New York: McGraw-Hill.

Weiss, A. (2003). *Great consulting challenges: And how to surmount them.* San Francisco: Jossey-Bass/Pfeiffer.

Wharton MBA Consulting Club. (1997). *The Wharton MBA case interview study guide.* San Francisco: WetFeet.

Wong, L. (2001). *The Harvard Business School guide to careers in management consulting,* Boston: Harvard Business School Press.

Subscribe to These Periodicals

Consultant News, www.consultant-news.com

Fortune Magazine, www.fortune.com

Harvard Business Review, www.HBR.org

T&D Journal, www.ASTD.org/TD/

Training Magazine, www.trainingmag.com

Wall Street Journal, www.WSJ.com

Electronic Resources

General Consulting Information

- Find general consulting support at the Association of Professional Consultants: www.consultapc.org.

- Stay abreast with the consulting industry at www.Kennedyinformation.com.

- Find an industry magazine at www.consultingmag.com.

- Contact the Institute of Management Consultants at www.IMCUSA.org.

General Business Information

- The Small Business Administration is a resource for general information such as financial planning: www.sba.gov.

- Looking for entrepreneurial support? Go to www.entrepreneurs.about.com.

- Trying to sort through the business etiquette in other countries? Get information at www.ExecutivePlanet.com, www.businesstravelogue.com, and www.cyborlink.com.

- Need copyright permission? Check www.copyright.com.

- Subscribe to an organizational ethics newsletter at www.ethics.org.

Start-Up Support

- Need help naming your business? Check out the software at www.namingtoolbox.com.

- Considering what insurance to purchase? Try http://www.iii.org/smallbusiness/intro/.

- Access tax considerations related to your business structure at www.IRS.gov.

- Software for writing a business plan can be found at www.business-plan.com.

- Wondering about salary expectations? Check one of these three sites: www.payscale.com, www.careerjournal.com, or www.salaryexpert.com.

- Look for opportunities to submit a proposal to the federal government at www.FedBizOpps.gov.

- Online survey support is available at www.zoomerang.com.

Call for Ideas

Want to be part of the next book on the business of consulting? If you are willing to share an idea or a story, please e-mail it to me at elaine@ebbweb.com. Your ideas will be compiled, and you will be given credit in an upcoming book.

Categories you may wish to consider include these:

- What start-up tips do you have for new consultants?
- What's your funniest consulting story?
- What's the most creative marketing tactic you've used?
- What issues or dilemmas do you run into the most often?

Call for Papers

Would you like to get your work published? How about submitting some of your good work to *Pfeiffer's Consulting Annual?* Possible topics for submissions include group and team building, organization development, leadership, problem solving, presentation and communication skills, consulting and facilitation, and train-the-trainer. Contributions may be in one of the following three formats:

- Experiential learning activities or structured experiences

- Inventories, questionnaires, or surveys

- Presentations and articles

Contact me to have a submission packet e-mailed (or snail-mailed) to you. The submission packet will help you determine format, language, and style to use, and it explains the submission requirements. You can reach me at elaine@ebbweb.com or ebboffice@aol.com. You may also call 757-588-3939.

elaine biech
consulting editor

About the Author

Elaine Biech is president and managing principal of ebb associates inc, an organizational development firm that helps organizations work through large-scale change. She has been in the training and consulting field for thirty years and works with business, government, and nonprofit organizations.

Elaine specializes in helping people work as teams to maximize their effectiveness. Customizing all of her work for individual clients, she conducts strategic planning sessions and implements corporatewide systems such as quality improvement, reengineering of business processes, and mentoring programs. She facilitates topics such as coaching employees, fostering creativity, customer service, time management, stress management, speaking skills, training competence, conducting productive meetings, managing change, handling difficult employees, organizational communication, conflict resolution, and effective listening.

She has presented at dozens of national and international conferences. Known as the trainer's trainer, she custom-designs training programs for managers, leaders, trainers, and consultants. Elaine has been featured in dozens of publications, including the *Wall Street Journal, Harvard Management Update*, the *Washington Post*, and *Fortune Magazine.*

As a management and executive consultant, trainer, and designer she has provided services to the Federal Aviation Administration, Land O' Lakes, McDonalds, Lands' End, General Casualty Insurance, Chrysler, Johnson Wax, Pricewaterhouse

Coopers, American Family Insurance, Marathon Oil, Hershey Chocolate, Federal Reserve Bank, the U.S. Navy, the National Aeronautics and Space Administration, Newport News Shipbuilding, Kohler Company, American Society for Training and Development (ASTD), American Red Cross, Association of Independent Certified Public Accountants, the University of Wisconsin, College of William and Mary, ODU, and hundreds of other public and private sector organizations.

She is the author and editor of over four dozen books and articles, including: *The Business of Consulting* (2nd ed., 2007), *Thriving Through Change: A Leader's Practical Guide to Change Mastery* (2007), *Successful Team-Building Tools* (2nd ed., 2007), *90 World-Class Activities by 90 World-Class Trainers* (2007; named a Training Review Best Training Product of 2007), the nine-volume set of *ASTD's Certification Study Guides* (2006), *Training for Dummies* (2005), *Marketing Your Consulting Services* (2003), *The Consultant's Legal Guide* (2000), and *The ASTD Sourcebook: Creativity and Innovation—Widen Your Spectrum* (1996). Her books have been translated into Chinese, German, and Dutch.

Elaine received her B.S. from the University of Wisconsin-Superior in business and education consulting and her M.S. in human resource development. She is active at the national level of ASTD: she is a lifetime member, served on the National ASTD board of directors, and was the International Conference Design chair in 2000. In addition, she has served on the Independent Consultants Association's Advisory Committee and the Instructional Systems Association board of directors.

Elaine is the recipient of the 1992 National ASTD Torch Award, the 2004 ASTD Volunteer-Staff Partnership Award, and the 2006 ASTD Gordon M. Bliss Memorial Award. She was selected for the 1995 Wisconsin Women Entrepreneurs' Mentor Award. In 2001 she received ISA's highest award, the ISA Spirit Award. She has been the consulting editor for the prestigious Training and Consulting Annuals published by Jossey-Bass/Pfeiffer for the past thirteen years.

Index

243

Pfeiffer Publications Guide

This guide is designed to familiarize you with the various types of Pfeiffer publications. The formats section describes the various types of products that we publish; the methodologies section describes the many different ways that content might be provided within a product. We also provide a list of the topic areas in which we publish.

FORMATS

In addition to its extensive book-publishing program, Pfeiffer offers content in an array of formats, from fieldbooks for the practitioner to complete, ready-to-use training packages that support group learning.

FIELDBOOK Designed to provide information and guidance to practitioners in the midst of action. Most fieldbooks are companions to another, sometimes earlier, work, from which its ideas are derived; the fieldbook makes practical what was theoretical in the original text. Fieldbooks can certainly be read from cover to cover. More likely, though, you'll find yourself bouncing around following a particular theme, or dipping in as the mood, and the situation, dictate.

HANDBOOK A contributed volume of work on a single topic, comprising an eclectic mix of ideas, case studies, and best practices sourced by practitioners and experts in the field.

  An editor or team of editors usually is appointed to seek out contributors and to evaluate content for relevance to the topic. Think of a handbook not as a ready-to-eat meal, but as a cookbook of ingredients that enables you to create the most fitting experience for the occasion.

RESOURCE Materials designed to support group learning. They come in many forms: a complete, ready-to-use exercise (such as a game); a comprehensive resource on one topic (such as conflict management) containing a variety of methods and approaches; or a collection of like-minded activities (such as icebreakers) on multiple subjects and situations.

TRAINING PACKAGE An entire, ready-to-use learning program that focuses on a particular topic or skill. All packages comprise a guide for the facilitator/trainer and a workbook for the participants. Some packages are supported with additional media—such as video—or learning aids, instruments, or other devices to help participants understand concepts or practice and develop skills.

- *Facilitator/trainer's guide* Contains an introduction to the program, advice on how to organize and facilitate the learning event, and step-by-step instructor notes. The guide also contains copies of presentation materials—handouts, presentations, and overhead designs, for example—used in the program.

- *Participant's workbook* Contains exercises and reading materials that support the learning goal and serves as a valuable reference and support guide for participants in the weeks and months that follow the learning event. Typically, each participant will require his or her own workbook.

ELECTRONIC CD-ROMs and web-based products transform static Pfeiffer content into dynamic, interactive experiences. Designed to take advantage of the searchability, automation, and ease-of-use that technology provides, our e-products bring convenience and immediate accessibility to your workspace.

METHODOLOGIES

CASE STUDY A presentation, in narrative form, of an actual event that has occurred inside an organization. Case studies are not prescriptive, nor are they used to prove a point; they are designed to develop critical analysis and decision-making skills. A case study has a specific time frame, specifies a sequence of events, is narrative in structure, and contains a plot structure—an issue (what should be/have been done?). Use case studies when the goal is to enable participants to apply previously learned theories to the circumstances in the case, decide what is pertinent, identify the real issues, decide what should have been done, and develop a plan of action.

ENERGIZER A short activity that develops readiness for the next session or learning event. Energizers are most commonly used after a break or lunch to stimulate or refocus the group. Many involve some form of physical activity, so they are a useful way to counter post-lunch lethargy. Other uses include transitioning from one topic to another, where "mental" distancing is important.

EXPERIENTIAL LEARNING ACTIVITY (ELA) A facilitator-led intervention that moves participants through the learning cycle from experience to application (also known as a Structured Experience). ELAs are carefully thought-out designs in which there is a definite learning purpose and intended outcome. Each step—everything that participants do during the activity—facilitates the accomplishment of the stated goal. Each ELA includes complete instructions for facilitating the intervention and a clear statement of goals, suggested group size and timing, materials required, an explanation of the process, and, where appropriate, possible variations to the activity. (For more detail on Experiential Learning Activities, see the Introduction to the *Reference Guide to Handbooks and Annuals*, 1999 edition, Pfeiffer, San Francisco.)

GAME A group activity that has the purpose of fostering team spirit and togetherness in addition to the achievement of a pre-stated goal. Usually contrived—undertaking a desert expedition, for example—this type of learning method offers an engaging means for participants to demonstrate and practice business and interpersonal skills. Games are effective for team building and personal development mainly because the goal is subordinate to the process—the means through which participants reach decisions, collaborate, communicate, and generate trust and understanding. Games often engage teams in "friendly" competition.

ICEBREAKER A (usually) short activity designed to help participants overcome initial anxiety in a training session and/or to acquaint the participants with one another. An icebreaker can be a fun activity or can be tied to specific topics or training goals. While a useful tool in itself, the icebreaker comes into its own in situations where tension or resistance exists within a group.

INSTRUMENT A device used to assess, appraise, evaluate, describe, classify, and summarize various aspects of human behavior. The term used to describe an instrument depends primarily on its format and purpose. These terms include survey, questionnaire, inventory, diagnostic, survey, and poll. Some uses of instruments include providing instrumental feedback to group members, studying here-and-now processes or functioning within a group, manipulating group composition, and evaluating outcomes of training and other interventions.

Instruments are popular in the training and HR field because, in general, more growth can occur if an individual is provided with a method for focusing specifically on his or her own behavior. Instruments also are used to obtain information that will serve as a basis for change and to assist in workforce planning efforts.

Paper-and-pencil tests still dominate the instrument landscape with a typical package comprising a facilitator's guide, which offers advice on administering the instrument and interpreting the collected data, and an initial set of instruments. Additional instruments are available separately. Pfeiffer, though, is investing heavily in e-instruments. Electronic instrumentation provides effortless distribution and, for larger groups particularly, offers advantages over paper-and-pencil tests in the time it takes to analyze data and provide feedback.

LECTURETTE A short talk that provides an explanation of a principle, model, or process that is pertinent to the participants' current learning needs. A lecturette is intended to establish a common language bond between the trainer and the participants by providing a mutual frame of reference. Use a lecturette as an introduction to a group activity or event, as an interjection during an event, or as a handout.

MODEL A graphic depiction of a system or process and the relationship among its elements. Models provide a frame of reference and something more tangible, and more easily remembered, than a verbal explanation. They also give participants something to "go on," enabling them to track their own progress as they experience the dynamics, processes, and relationships being depicted in the model.

ROLE PLAY A technique in which people assume a role in a situation/ scenario: a customer service rep in an angry-customer exchange, for example. The way in which the role is approached is then discussed and feedback is offered. The role play is often repeated using a different approach and/or incorporating changes made based on feedback received. In other words, role playing is a spontaneous interaction involving realistic behavior under artificial (and safe) conditions.

SIMULATION A methodology for understanding the interrelationships among components of a system or process. Simulations differ from games in that they test or use a model that depicts or mirrors some aspect of reality in form, if not necessarily in content. Learning occurs by studying the effects of change on one or more factors of the model. Simulations are commonly used to test hypotheses about what happens in a system—often referred to as "what if?" analysis—or to examine best-case/worst-case scenarios.

THEORY A presentation of an idea from a conjectural perspective. Theories are useful because they encourage us to examine behavior and phenomena through a different lens.

TOPICS

The twin goals of providing effective and practical solutions for workforce training and organization development and meeting the educational needs of training and human resource professionals shape Pfeiffer's publishing program. Core topics include the following:

Leadership & Management

Communication & Presentation

Coaching & Mentoring

Training & Development

E-Learning

Teams & Collaboration

OD & Strategic Planning

Human Resources

Consulting

What will you find on pfeiffer.com?

- The best in workplace performance solutions for training and HR professionals

- Downloadable training tools, exercises, and content

- Web-exclusive offers

- Training tips, articles, and news

- Seamless on-line ordering

- Author guidelines, information on becoming a Pfeiffer Affiliate, and much more

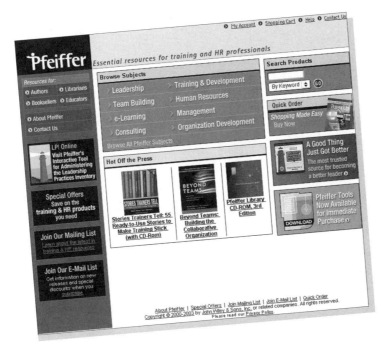

Discover more at www.pfeiffer.com